BLUE EXORCIST 12

KAZUE KATO

Contents 12

Cast of Characters

Rin Okumura

Born of a human mother and Satan, the God of Demons, Rin Okumura has powers he can barely control. After Satan kills Father Fujimoto, Rin's foster father, Rin decides to become an Exorcist so he can someday defeat Satan. Now a first-year student at True Cross Academy and an Exwire at the Exorcism Cram School, he hopes to someday become a Knight. When he draws the Koma Sword, he manifests his infernal power in the form of blue flames. He succeeded in defeating the Impure King and affirmed his determination to live with his flame.

Yukio Okumura

Rin's brother. Hoping to become a doctor, he's a genius who is the youngest student ever to become an instructor at the Exorcism Cram School. An instructor in Demon Pharmaceuticals, he possesses the titles of Doctor and Dragoon. Todo told him that his true nature is that of a demon.

Shiemi Moriyama

Daughter of the owner of Futsumaya, an Exorcist supply shop. She possesses the ability to become a Tamer and can summon a baby Greenman named Nee. She passed the high school entrance exam, so now she is a classmate of Rin and the others.

Ryuji Suguro

Heir to the venerable Buddhist sect known as Myodha in Kyoto. He is an Exwire who hopes to become an Exorcist someday so he can reestablish his family's temple, which fell on hard times after the Blue Night. He wants to achieve the titles of Dragoon and Aria.

Renzo Shima

Once a pupil of Suguro's father and now Suguro's friend. He's an Exwire who wants to become an Aria. He has an easygoing personality and is totally girl-crazy.

Konekomaru Miwa

Like Shima, he was once a pupil of Suguro's father and is now Suguro's friend. He's an Exwire who hopes to become an Exorcist someday. He is small in size and has a quiet and composed personality.

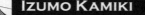

Izumo Kamiki

An Exwire with the blood of shrine maidens. She has the ability to become a Tamer and can summon two white foxes.

Noriko Paku

An old friend of Kamiki's. They entered the Exorcism Cram School together, but she couldn't keep up with classes and dropped out. She is currently attending regular classes at True Cross Academy High School.

Nemu Takara

A student at the Exorcism Cram School. He is a puppet master who can summon and control dolls. Mephisto played a role in his acceptance to True Cross Academy.

Shura Kirigakure

An upper-rank special investigator dispatched by Vatican Headquarters to True Cross Academy. She's a Senior Exorcist First Class who holds the titles of Knight, Tamer, Doctor and Aria. She used to be Father Fujimoto's pupil.

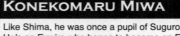

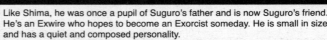

MEPHISTO PHELES

President of True Cross Academy and head of the Exorcism Cram School. He was Father Fujimoto's friend, and now he is Rin and Yukio's guardian. He is the second power in Gehenna and known as Samael, King of Time.

ARTHUR A. ANGEL

A Senior Exorcist First Class and the current Paladin. He wields the demon sword Caliban and is certain that Rin, as the bearer of Satan's blood, should be destroyed.

LEWIN LIGHT

A Senior Exorcist First Class with a deep knowledge of demons. He speaks to the current Paladin, Arthur, as an equal and appears to occupy a high position within the Order.

KURO

A Cat Sídhe who was once Shiro's familiar. After Shiro's death, he began turning back into a demon. Rin saved him, and now the two are practically inseparable. His favorite drink is the catnip wine Shiro used to make.

The Story So Far

Unknown to Rin Okumura, both human and demon blood runs in his veins. In an argument with his foster father, Father Fujimoto, Rin learns that Satan is his true father. Satan suddenly appears and tries to drag Rin down to Gehenna because Rin has inherited his power. Father Fujimoto fights to defend Rin, but dies in the process. Rin decides to become an Exorcist so he can someday defeat Satan and begins studying at the Exorcism Cram School under the instruction of his twin brother Yukio, who is already an Exorcist.

Rin and the others succeed in defeating the Impure King, awakened by the former exorcist, Todo. Meanwhile, Yukio fights Todo, and as the battle rages, he senses the same flame in his own eyes as his brother. Afraid, he keeps it a secret.

Rin returns to school life at True Cross Academy, but his classmate Godaiin suddenly starts seeing demons during summer break. In fact, reports of such mysterious incidents have been coming in from around the globe, with the Impure Princess returning in Yemen and a man-made Gehenna Gate appearing in Russia.

The secret society known as the Illuminati is behind these events. An investigation reveals that the organization has spies within the Knights of the True Cross and one of the spies has infiltrated True Cross Academy. Nothing has happened yet, but the Illuminati is increasingly active in the days leading up to the academy festival.

Meanwhile, Shiemi passes the academy entrance exam and Rin is thrilled to have her as a classmate. On the day of the academy festival, in the shadows of all the excitement, the Illuminati makes its move!!

Chapter 48: The Night Of The True Cross Academy Festival

I finally appeared in full color! But it's black-and-white in the graphic novel...
Yeah...

WAAAAH

ANSWER ME!!!

...IN THE *ILLUMINATI?!*

GYAAAAAH

KOFF

KOFF

KOFF

COME ON! CONFESS!
ILLUMINATI SCUM!!
ARTHUR, LET ME TALK TO HIM...
...BEFORE YOU BLUDGEON HIM TO DEATH WITH YOUR ANGER!
AS YOU CAN SEE, HE DOESN'T RESPOND TO DEALS...
...OR PHYSICAL PUNISHMENT!
THERE'S ANOTHER SPY...

KCHNK
...SO I DON'T MIND IF THIS ONE DIES.
?!
WHAT WAS THAT?

THE DOORS WON'T OPEN!!
WHAT ?!
WE'RE LOCKED IN.

W
THE OTHER SPY MUST HAVE DONE THIS.

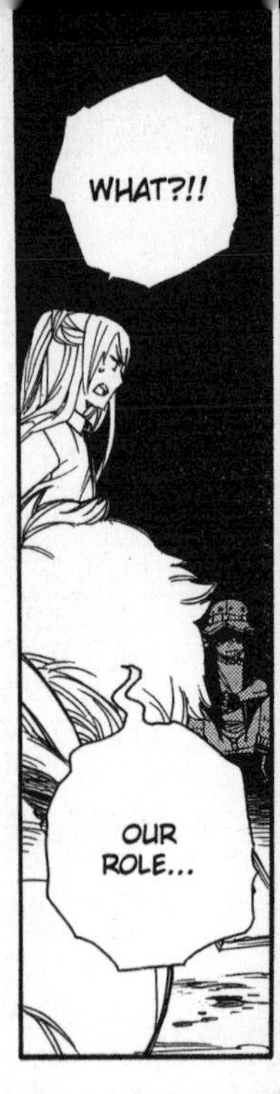
WHAT?!!
OUR ROLE...

...IS TO KEEP YOU HERE.

AH, I SEE...
YOU DON'T WANT US INTERFERING WITH THE BIG EVENT...
...THAT'S ABOUT TO START.
YOU AREN'T INVITED.

DOWN HERE, YOU CAN'T CONTACT ANYONE OUTSIDE.

SO YOU GET TO COOL YOUR HEELS UNTIL IT'S ALL OVER.

I WOULD LOVE TO, BUT...

...THE PEOPLE OF TRUE CROSS ABSOLUTELY *LOVE* SPECIAL EVENTS!

GRRR

!

GO, SALAMANDER!!!

GYAAH!

WE'VE CAPTURED A SPY!!

WE'RE OPENING THE DOORS!!

KLACK
ARE YOU ALL RIGHT?
THAT WAS QUICK.
WELL DONE.
!!!!

YOU SAW THE WHOLE THING COMING?!
WHY DIDN'T YOU TELL ME?!
BECAUSE YOU'RE A TERRIBLE LIAR.
GAH
WELL, YEAH!!
WE BROUGHT THEM, LIGHTNING!

DEAR ...?
PAPA!!
NOW LET'S GET DOWN TO BUSINESS.
YOU HAVE FAILED IN YOUR "ROLE."
WHAT'S GOING ON HERE?!

SO, TELL ME ABOUT THIS "BIG EVENT" THAT'S ABOUT TO BEGIN.

BASTARD!

OH MY! ATTITUDE, HUH?

SHALL I ASK YOUR WIFE AND SON?

NO!

THEY DON'T KNOW ANYTHING!

DON'T ACT LIKE YOU'RE INNOCENT!

WE'RE BOTH BASTARDS, SO DON'T MAKE ME LAUGH!

...LET'S SO... GET STARTED.

PAPA!

EEK! WHAT ARE YOU DOING?!

W...

WITHIN ONE HOUR, WE'RE GOING TO KIDNAP A GIRL AT THE JAPAN BRANCH!

A GIRL WHO'S IMPORTANT TO OUR SOCIETY'S PLANS!!

WHAT'S HER NAME?

IZUMO KAMIKI!

THEY'LL FIND US HERE IN NO TIME.
HUP
IF YOU WANT TO KNOW, FOLLOW ME.
?!
HURRY!
...!
TMP
URGH!

BEEEP
BEEEP
YEAH? DID YOU LEARN ANYTHING?
HUH?
KAMIKI?!

CLIK
BEEP
WHAT?
HEY...
...

NO WAY!
BIP
BIP
BIP

BEEP BEEP
YES?
SHURA?

HUH?
FOO WIF IT?

FIND IZUMO KAMIKI.

HUH?! WHAT HAPPENED TO HER?!

I ASKED HER...

...TO WORK AT OUR BOOTH TONIGHT...

...BUT SHE DIDN'T COME.

IS SHE ALL RIGHT?

I DON'T KNOW.

I'LL EXPLAIN LATER.

FOR NOW, JUST FIND HER AS SOON AS POSSIBLE.

AND WE CAN'T REACH NEMU TAKARA EITHER. FIND HIM TOO.

WILL THE CRAM SCHOOL STUDENTS BE ENOUGH?

SHOULDN'T WE CONTACT THE INSTRUCTORS...

...AND LORD PHEL-

NO!

TREAT THIS AS A TOP-SECRET ASSIGNMENT FROM VATICAN HEADQUARTERS.

DO ***NOT*** INFORM MEPHISTO!

...

COVER MORE GROUND BY SPLITTING UP.
AND STAY IN TOUCH.

THAT'S ALL! NOW GET TO IT!

HURRY!!

WAAAH

OH NO! WHAT HAPPENED TO IZUMO?!

LET'S SPLIT UP THE SEARCH AREA.

W
THERE'S NO TIME FOR THAT!!
SHIMA!! CONTROL YOURSELF!!
AAAA
WE'LL BE TOO LATE TO SAVE IZUMO!
H
SHIEMI...
...THIS HEADSET WILL CONNECT YOU TO MS. KIRIGAKURE.

THANK YOU!
I'LL GO ASK PAKU!
They're roomies!
GOOD IDEA!

I'LL SEARCH SCHOOL AREAS.
I'LL GO CLOCKWISE FROM THE NORTH GATE.
I'LL GO THE OPPOSITE DIRECTION OF BON.
I'LL SEE IF SHE SHOWED UP AT THE SHOP...
...AND SEARCH AROUND THE ARCADE.
Crepe
DON'T LOSE CONTROL, RIN.
I WON'T!!

WE SHOULD BE FINE HERE.
HUFF
HUFF
...

HOW DID YOU GET THAT DOLL?

...

HAVE YOU DONE SOMETHING TO TSUKUMO?!

NOTHING.
TOSS

WHAP
!

TSUKUMO ENTRUSTED THAT TO ME.
TAKE GOOD CARE OF IT.
TSUKUMO GAVE IT TO YOU?!

THAT CAN'T BE!!
IT'S A CHARM I GAVE TSUKUMO TO KEEP AT ALL TIMES!
TSUKUMO WOULD NEVER GIVE IT TO YOU!!
WHO ARE YOU?!!

POK

I AM A COORDINATOR.

COORDINATOR ?!

I OBSERVE YOU GUYS...

...AND COORDINATE TO MAKE SURE THINGS GO SMOOTHLY.

OF ALL THE TIMES! I'M NOT PREPARED FOR A FIGHT!!

I ONLY HAVE ONE SET OF SEALS...
SHF
...TO TAKE ON THIS STRONG OPPONENT ?!
DON'T.

POK
MY EMPLOYER ASKED ME NOT TO HARM YOU.
POK
I HAVE NO CHOICE! HERE GOES!
FWIP
THEN FIGHT WITHOUT HARMING ME!
THAT WOULD HELP A LOT!!
"I HUMBLY BESEECH THEE..."
"...TO GRANT MY REQUEST!"
FWH

TCH!
"COME FORTH!"
"SUPER MECH WARRIOR: SENTOGAIA!"
BWUP
BWUP
"TRANSFORMING ROBOT TOY!"
"1/18 MODEL ENLARGED!!!"
POOF
!!!!
SHUF SHUF
NO ONE SAID ANYTHING ABOUT THIS!!!!
CLAP
CLAP
WE DON'T DO WELL AGAINST PLASTIC!
DON'T RUN!!
"FURUE YURAYURAFURUE YURAYURATO FURUE!!"

"EXPEL-"
WHSH
BWSH
BWSH
SENTOGAIA ROCKET PUNCH!
FIRE!!!
POW
...!
POW
CHOK
CHOK
YOU SHOULDN'T PESTER ADUL-
HWSH
!
BWSH
SENTOGAIA MISSILE PUNCH!
FIRE!!

NO WAY!
I THOUGHT YOU WEREN'T ALLOWED TO HARM ME!!
KLANG
YOU BAD, BAD BOY!

PLAY NICE WITH MY DEAR IZUMO!!
PINK-HEAD...
I GOT HERE FIRST! IT'S FATE! ♡
Right?
BUT WAIT... I'M SUPPOSED TO CALL MS. KIRI-
FORGET ABOUT IT, YOU BRAT!
POK
POK
POK
YOU LEAVE ME NO CHOICE...
HEY!

CLOMP
"ON..."
"...GIRISHUCHIRI BIKIRI..."
CLOMP CLOMP CLOMP
?!
"...TADANOUUN SARABASHADORO DASHAYA..."
"...SATANBAYA SATANBAYA..."
Eek!
TOMP
"...SOHATTA SOHATTA SOUKA"!!
FW OSH
GIMME A LITTLE HELP HERE...
YAMANTAKA!

I'VE BEEN WAITING! SO I'M READY FOR A RUMBLE!
YAMANTAKA?!!
YOU...
THAT'S A HIGH-LEVEL MYO-O DEMON!!
WHAM
WHEN DID YOU GET SUCH A POWERFUL DEMON FAMILIAR?!
UM...

WHEN I WAS A KID.

BUT IT TIRES ME OUT...

...SO I RARELY USE IT.

RESCUING YOU IS DIFFERENT, THOUGH! ♡

YOU TRICKY DOG!! PUT ME DOWN!

BA BIP BIP BIP

A CHILD'S TOY?

BURN IN HELLFIRE!

WHAT'S THAT BLACK FLAME?!

IT'S FROM GEHENNA AND DIFFERENT FROM THE RED KIND, WHICH IS PHYSICAL.
IF YOU EXPEL A DEMON WITH A PHYSICAL FLAME...
...YOU JUST DESTROY THE PHYSICAL VESSEL, RIGHT?
BOOM
THE DEMON JUST ENTERS A DIFFERENT VESSEL.

KLAK
BUT THIS BLACK FLAME LEAVES THE VESSEL UNTOUCHED WHILE DESTROYING THE DEMON INSIDE!

LIKE THE FLAME OF SATAN?
NO.
THAT'S A SPECIAL FLAME THAT CAN AFFECT BOTH.
POOF
POOF
POOF
POOF
POOF
"COME FORTH, KNIFE RABBITS! PRODUCTION MODEL STUFFED ANIMALS!"

"QUANTITY: 100!!!"
GNASH
GRAR
SNARL
!!!
KYAAH!
GRAR
YAMANTAKA! GET THEM!!
GNASH
SNARL
GRAR
KATSU!
BO
DAIITOKU, UNLEASH YOUR WRATH!

KATO KONGO SPEAR!!!
FWSH
THUP
SPIN
!!
WACK
TH

UGH!
WHAM
...!!!
HUFF
HUFF
IF I USE THIS BLACK FLAME ON PEOPLE...
...IT WON'T HURT THEIR BODIES...
...BUT IT WILL BURN THEIR SOULS!!
"ON..."
"AKU..."
"...UN"!!

NEMU!
...!!
SHIVR

...!
AIEE!

WSH

WHA...
WHAT HAPPENED?!

...

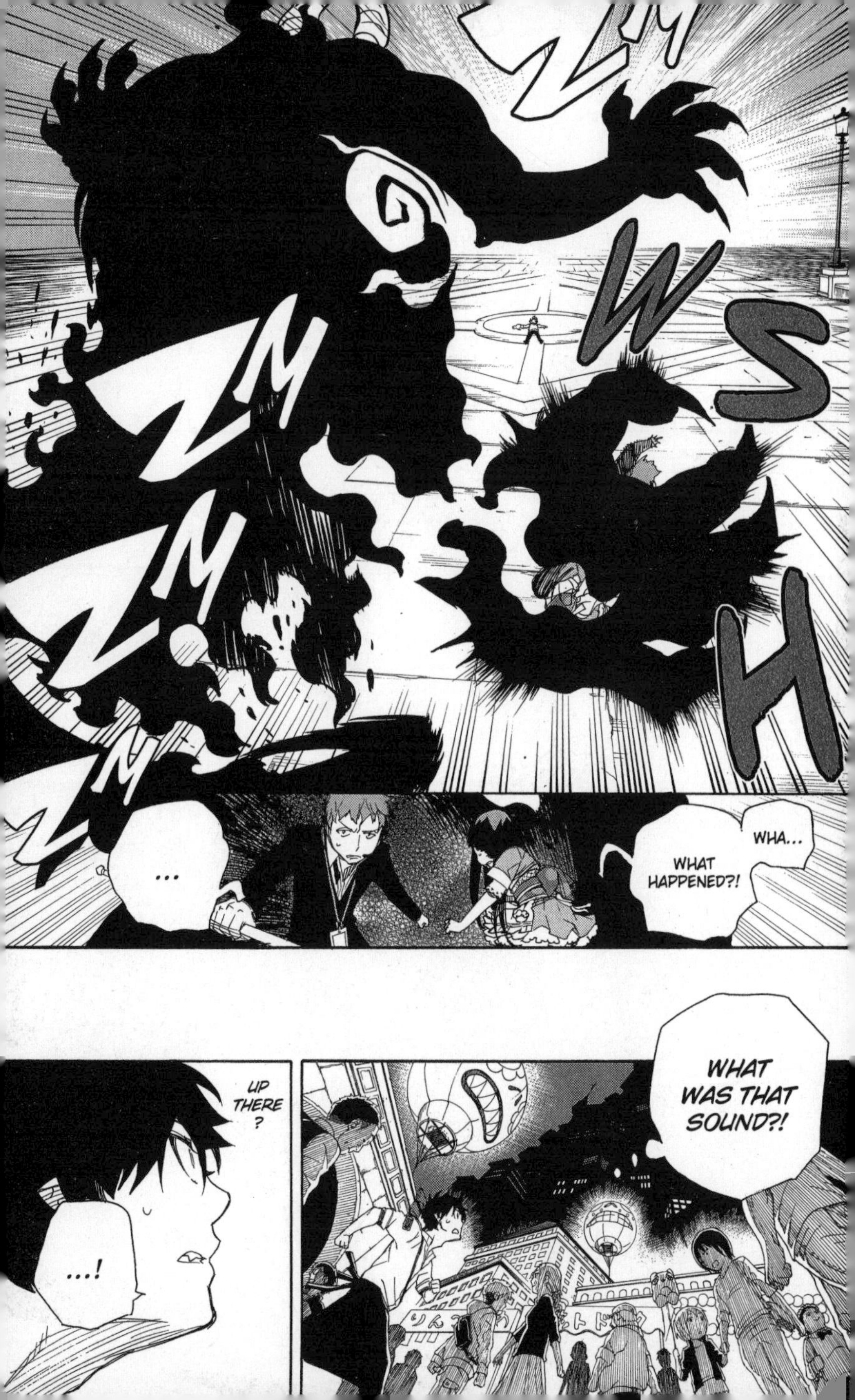

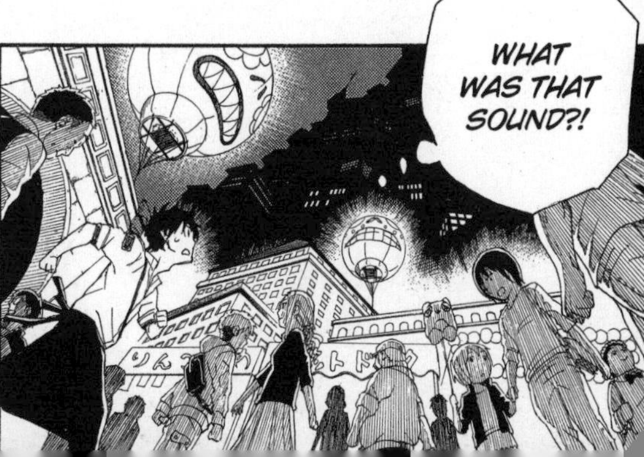
WHAT WAS THAT SOUND?!

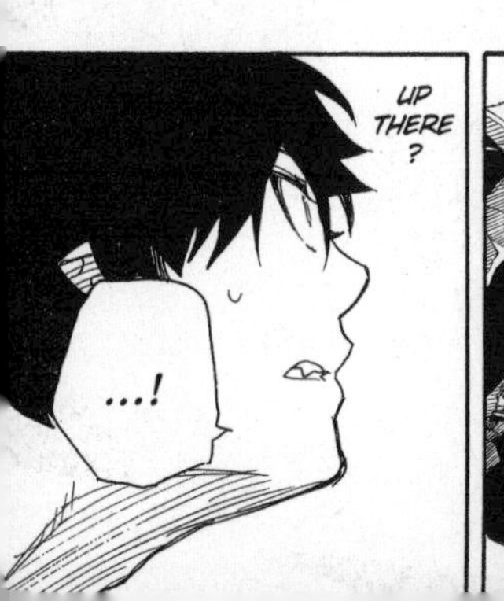
UP THERE?
...!

RR
CALM DOWN, NEMU...
MM
GO TO SLEEP...
MM

RMM
WE DON'T KNOW WHAT WE'RE UP AGAINST!
A PAWN OF LORD PHELES?

IZUMO!
HERE! GIVE ME YOUR–
!
SLAP
I'M DONE BEING A BURDEN!
I'LL GO CALL FOR HELP!

I CAN'T ALLOW THAT.
SH
UK

IF ANYTHING HAPPENS TO YOU, MY SUPERIORS WON'T BE PLEASED.

SHLUF

IT'S ALL RIGHT.

...SO HANG IN THERE.
AHA...
...NOW I SEE.

YOU'RE THE ILLUMINATI SPY?

Blue Exorcist Chapter 48: The Night of the True Cross Academy Festival

Chapter 49: True Cross Academy Festival—The Final Night
WHAT IS THIS FEELING?
EVERYONE!!
MR. OKUMURA!
SHURA, SHIMA AND RIN STILL AREN'T HERE?!!
YEAH...
SOME-THING'S COMING !!
MAYBE THEY DIDN'T HEAR THE SUMMONS.
WHOOSH
RIN ??!!

Chapter 49:
True Cross
Academy
Festival—The
Final Night

YOU'RE THE ILLUMINATI SPY?
HUH?
NO, NO, NO!
CALLING ME A "SPY" IS AN EXAGGERATION!
I JUST OBSERVE THE EXORCISM CRAM SCHOOL STUDENTS.
WUP
WUP
WUP
WUP
HM?
WUP
WUP
WUP
WUP
I ONLY RECENTLY GOT MY FIRST REAL ASSIGNMENT.

WUP
WUP
WUP
WUP
THAT WOULD BE MY *BOSS*...
VRR
VRR

TMP
VRR

VRR
VRR

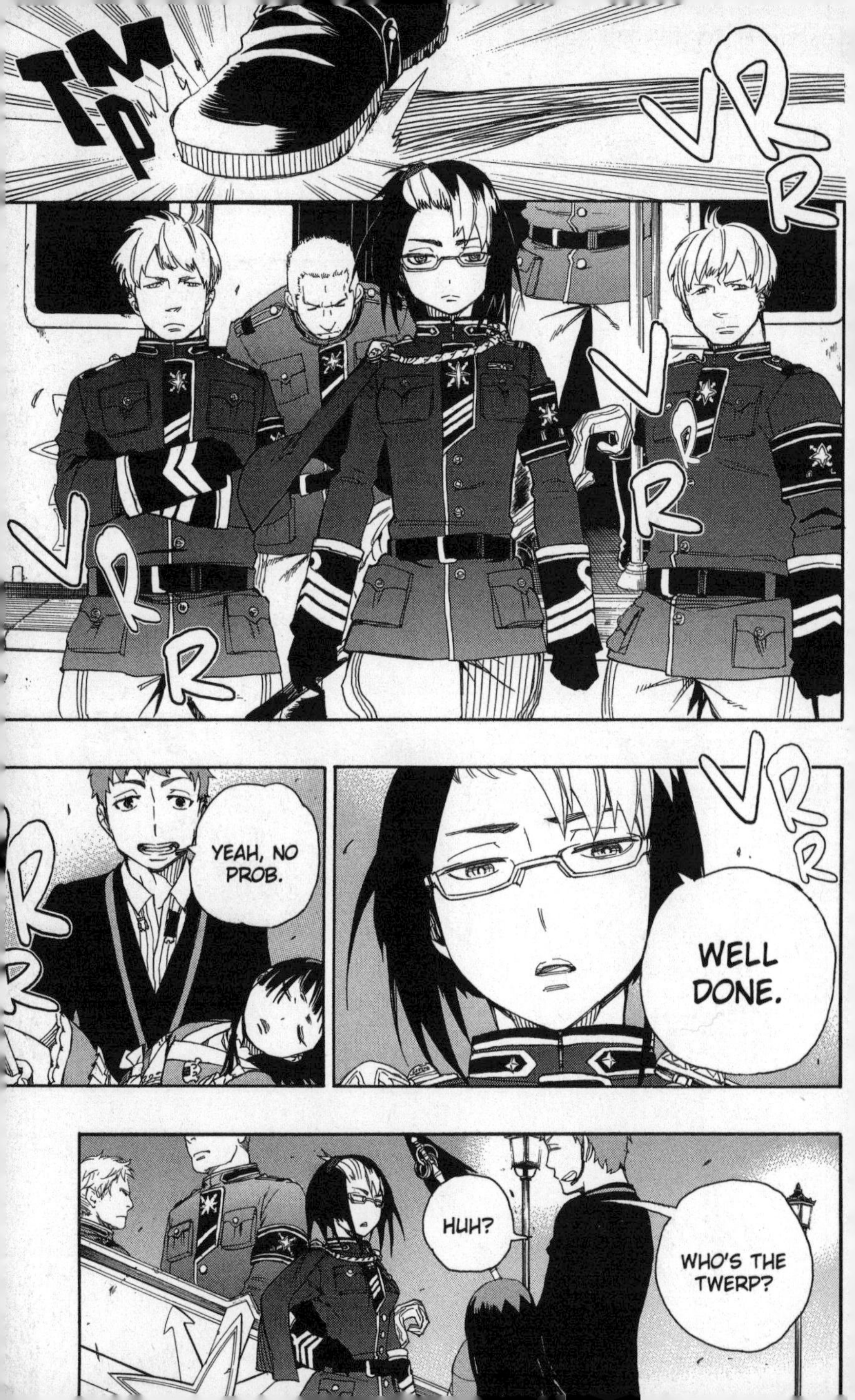

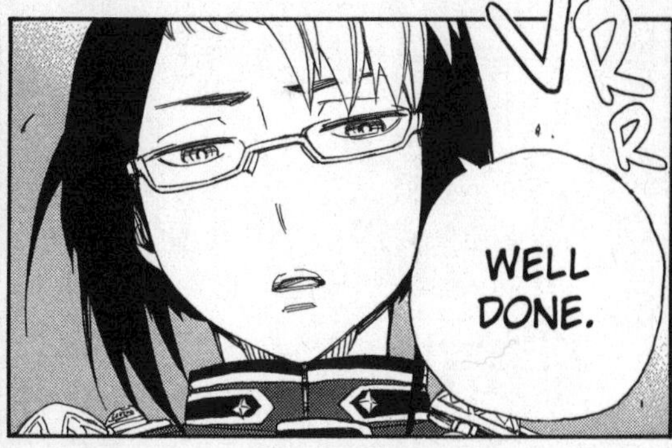
VRR
WELL DONE.

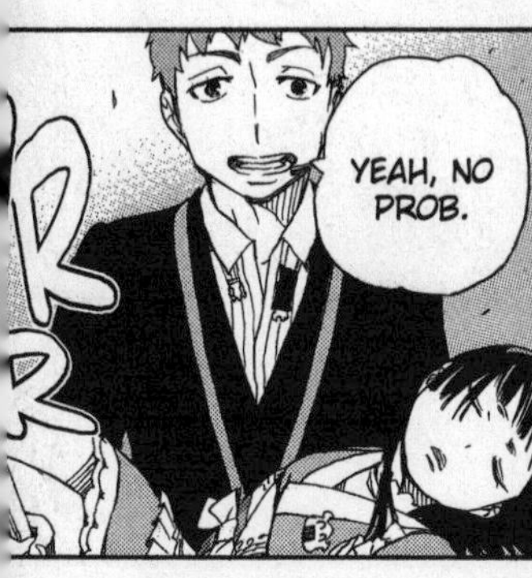
YEAH, NO PROB.

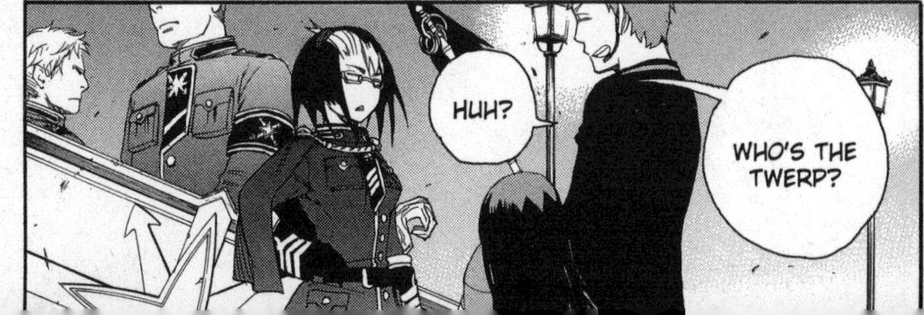
WHO'S THE TWERP?
HUH?

OH, UH...
...

POK POK
I ACHIEVED MY GOAL. I WILL NOT INTERFERE.

NO WORRIES THEN! ♥
...

WHAM
WHAM
WHAM
UM...
...WHAT'S ALL THIS?
YOU'RE NOT LEAVING?

BE CAREFUL NOT TO FLUB THIS UP.
HEY, WAIT A-
SHIMA!!

!!
IZUMO?!
ANGEL, YOU AIRHEAD!
YOU'RE TOO SLOW!! SEND BACKUP!!
DON'T WORRY.
WE'LL BE IN JAPAN IN THIRTY SECONDS. ONCE I'M THERE, NOTHING CAN-

UGH! WHAT IS THAT?!

...!!

?!

N-NO WAY...

E
R
V
SERAPHIM...
E
E
KIN OF THE KING OF LIGHT!!
E
SHIMA!!!

HE HAS COME.

BAWHAM
WHAT THE?!
IT'S HOT!
POOF
MNCH MNCH
MEPHISTO!

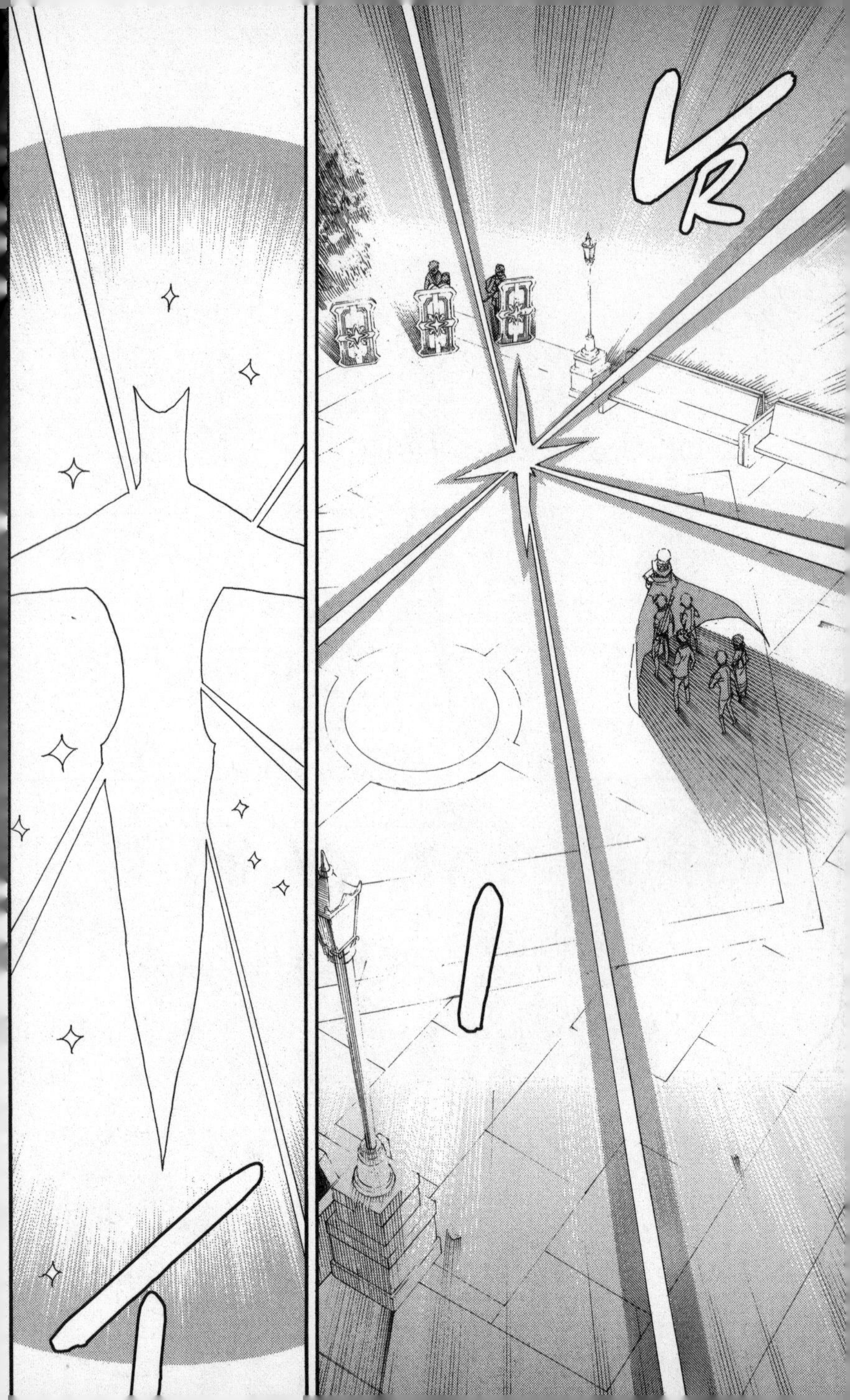
VR

IT IS A PLEASURE...

...TO MEET ALL OF YOU.

PLEASE FORGIVE ME...
...FOR SO FORCEFULLY MAKING MYSELF HEARD.
?!
THE SERAPHIM IS SPEAKING!!
THIS VOICE...
OH, I GET IT. THE SERAPHIM SPEAK FOR THE ILLUMINATI.

THEY MUST WANT TO PRESENT THEIR MANIFESTO TO THE WORLD. THE SERAPHIM MAY BE APPEARING BEFORE THE GRIGORI AS WELL.
WHAT?!
MY, MY...

...I NEVER THOUGHT THEIR BIG EVENT WOULD BE *THIS* BIG.

POOF

POOF

SWIP

I AM THE COMMANDER-IN-CHIEF OF THE ILLUMINATI.

I AM *LUCIFER,* THE KING OF LIGHT.

MY BIG BROTHER!
IT SEEMS WHILE WE WERE APART YOU...HEE HEE HEE... ANYWAY, THE MASK SUITS YOU!
SWIP

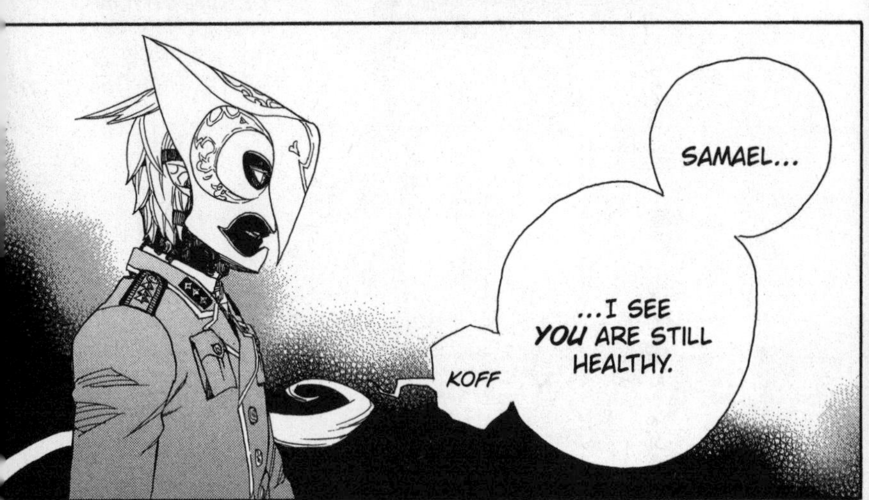
SAMAEL...
...I SEE *YOU* ARE STILL HEALTHY.
KOFF

THANKS TO YOU, I'M HAVING A BLAST.
WHAT? HE'S SHAKING...
QUIVER
BUT WHAT BRINGS YOU TO THIS LITTLE BACKWATER?
WELL...

...AS A FIRST STEP, WE IN THE ILLUMINATI...
...HAVE COME TO ISSUE A DECLARATION OF WAR AGAINST THE KNIGHTS OF THE TRUE CROSS.
IN LESS THAN ONE YEAR FROM THIS DAY...
...WE WILL REVIVE OUR FATHER, SATAN!

WE WILL REJOIN ASSIAH AND GEHENNA AS *ONE...*
...AND RETURN TO THE NOTHINGNESS THAT PRECEDED DARKNESS AND LIGHT.
THEN ALL WILL BE FREE OF SUFFERING, TO EXIST IN EQUALITY AND HARMONY.
THE WORLD WILL KNOW *TRUE PEACE.*

THE ILLUMINATI WILL NOT FORGIVE ANY WHO OPPOSE OUR WILL.

HOW-EVER...

...THE DOOR IS ALWAYS OPEN TO THOSE WHO WOULD LISTEN.

SAMAEL...

AS YOUR OLDER BROTHER, I ASK YOU ONE LAST TIME...

...WILL YOU JOIN ME IN–

HEH

BA

NEVER.

LIVING ATOP A PILE OF CORPSES, LONGING FOR THE SKY WHILE CRAWLING THROUGH A WORLD OF SUFFERING...

...AND THE CHAOS OF DIFFERENT BEINGS EXISTING SIDE BY SIDE... *THAT'S* MY IDEA OF PEACE!

BUT WHY MUST WE...

...LIVE IN SIN AND AGONY?

NOT ALL IN THIS WORLD ARE AS STRONG AS YOU.

MANY ARE WEAK.

PLIP

WE JUST SEE THE WORLD DIFFERENTLY, BRO!
SO IT SEEMS.

AND YOU HAVE YOUR OWN IDEAS AS WELL...
GLANCE
JOLT
THEN LET US NOT HOLD ANYTHING BACK AND EACH GIVE OUR BEST.
BY THE WAY, I'M TAKING THE GIRL.
SHE IS NECESSARY TO OUR PLANS.

TAK
NOW IF YOU'LL PARDON ME...
TAK
STAGGER
FWUD
COMMANDER !!
KOFF KOFF
KOFF
CALL A DOCTOR!!
OH... OKAY.
YOU'RE COMING WITH US, SHIMA!
!!
W...
WAIT!!
WHAT'RE YOU GONNA DO WITH IZUMO AND SHIMA?!

HEY! MEPHISTO!!! ARE YOU JUST GOING TO STAND THERE AND WATCH?!
WHAT CAN I DO AGAINST THE KING OF LIGHT?
HE MAY BE WEAKENED, BUT HE'S GEHENNA'S GREATEST POWER!
...
BUT YOU SHOULD HAVE SENSED THAT, RIGHT?
WELL THEN...
RIN?!
FW
...I'LL STOP HIM!!

GO.
TUMP
HWOOSH
??!
SHIMA...
OKUMURA.
KLANG
I'M WARNING YOU...
...YOU CAN'T WIN THIS UNLESS YOU'RE READY TO BE A *KILLER*...
...BECAUSE THE ILLUMINATI ARE MORTAL HUMANS.

KLANG
IS THIS A *JOKE,* SHIMA?
!!
COME BACK TO US!!!
RAM
HA!

THANKS FOR TRUSTING ME, GUYS!

BUT *THIS*...

...IS WHO I AM.

SEE YA!

VRR
VRR
GRAH
BON...
SHIMA!
IS THAT ALL...
...HE CAN SAY?!
VRR
RENZOOO!

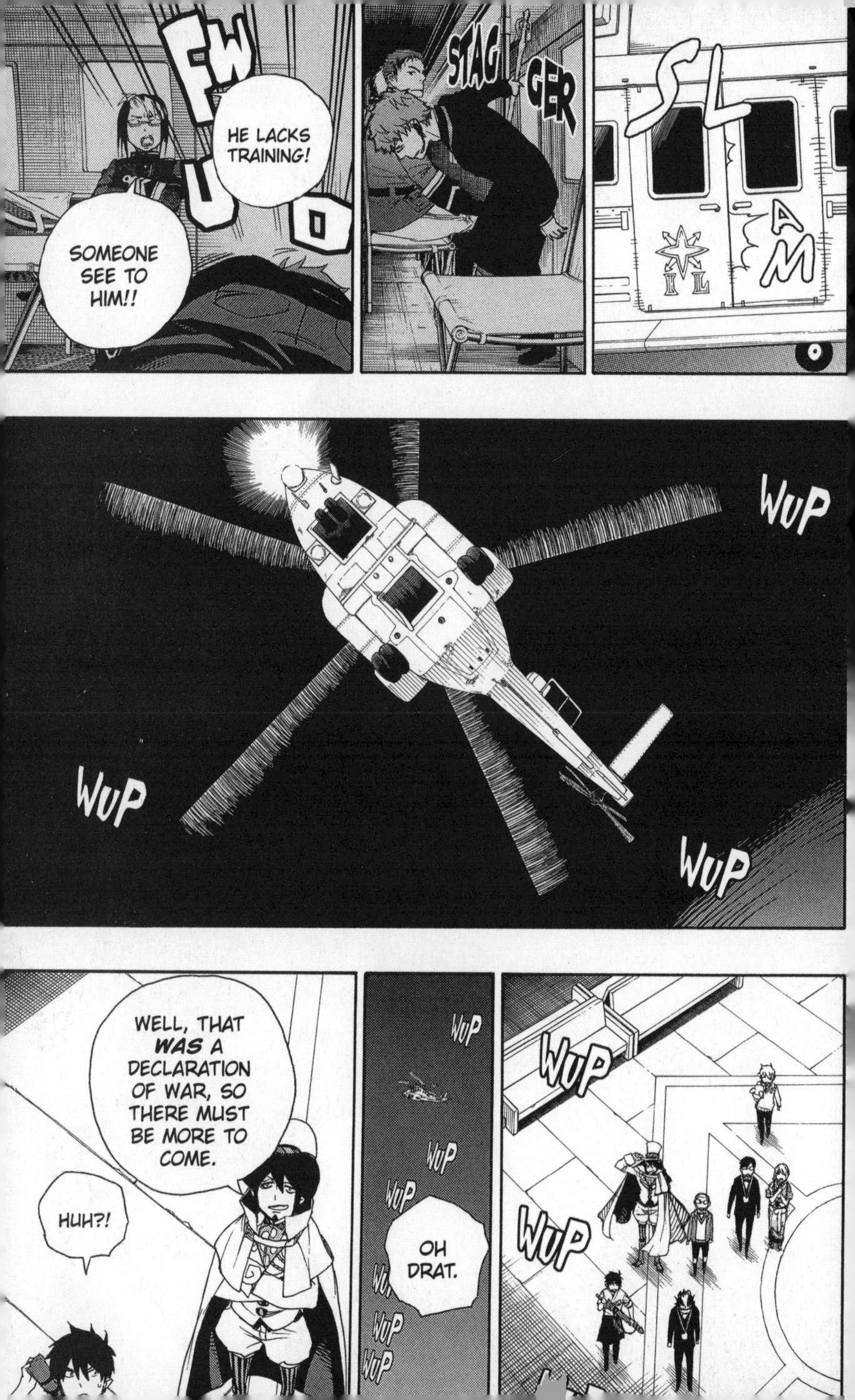

SLAM
STAGGER
HE LACKS TRAINING!
SOMEONE SEE TO HIM!!
FWUD

WUP

WUP

WUP

WUP
WUP

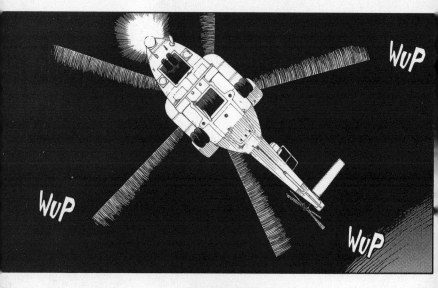

WUP
WUP
WUP
OH DRAT.
WUP
WUP

WELL, THAT *WAS* A DECLARATION OF WAR, SO THERE MUST BE MORE TO COME.
HUH?!

SEIJYUJI PARK

GYAH!
WHAM
RR
THE GRIGORI!!!
THEY CERTAINLY HAVE SEIZED THE INITIATIVE.
MMM
AAAAH! GYAAAAH!
WAAAH

RR
THE KING OF LIGHT DESTROYED THE MAIN BARRIER EARLIER.
THE EXPLODING SERAPHIM DESTROYED THE SMALLER BARRIERS.
M
MM
BEHOLD!
M
M
LOW-LEVEL...
NO, MID-LEVEL DEMONS ARE GATHERING!

FROM THE LOOKS OF THINGS...
...I WOULD GUESS THE OTHER BRANCHES AROUND THE WORLD ARE IN A SIMILAR STATE OF CONFUSION.
I MUST SEE TO THE JAPAN BRANCH.
INTERMEDIATE EXORCIST FIRST CLASS, YUKIO OKUMURA!
!!
YES?
TAKE CHARGE OF THE EXWIRES...
...AND IMMEDIATELY GO TO RESCUE IZUMO KAMIKI.

J-JUST ME AND SOME EXWIRES?!

WHEN THINGS ARE UNDER CONTROL HERE, I'LL SEND BACKUP.
BESIDES, NEMU TAKARA WILL GO WITH YOU.
?
BUT WHO *IS* HE?!

HE'S AN EXORCIST I BROUGHT IN FROM OUTSIDE...
...TO SUPERVISE YOU CRAM SCHOOL STUDENTS.
WHAT ?!
HE HAS SENIOR FIRST CLASS ABILITY, SO DON'T WORRY.
HE KNOWS WHERE TO GO.
...
WHAT ABOUT SHIMA?

IT'S MY FAULT FOR NOT INVESTIGATING HIM MORE THOROUGHLY.
I HAVE NO EXCUSE.
BUT FOR NOW, WE MUST ACCEPT...
...THAT HE WAS A *RAT* FOR THE ILLUMI-
GWA
B
GURK?!
SHUT UP!!
DON'T SAY THAT, *CLOWN*!

SHIKR
WE STILL CAN'T BE SURE!!!!
WE'LL FIND IZUMO AND SHIMA...
...AND WE'RE GONNA BRING 'EM BACK!!

Blue Exorcist Chapter 49: True Cross Academy Festival—The Final Night

DRIP
DRIP
HELP ME...
DRIP

Chapter 50: The Most Important Thing to Me

WAKE UP!

SNAP

!

HUH? DID I...

DID I PASS OUT?!

Pee-yew!

WEAKLING.

...

WELL, I HAVEN'T SUMMONED ANYTHING FOR A WHILE...
...SO IT WENT STRAIGHT TO MY HEAD.
WHERE ARE WE?

THE FAR EAST LABORATORY.
PUT THIS ON.
FUMP
LISTEN.
RRIP
YOU'RE WORTHLESS ASIDE FROM YOUR MYO-O DEMON.

HOW'S IZUMO KAMIKI?
SHE'S IN CONFINEMENT. I'M ON MY WAY TO TALK TO HER.
YOU SHOULD WRITE A REPORT AND–
OH? THEN YOU'LL NEED ME! ♪
?

LEAVE IZUMO TO ME!
I'VE HAD MY EYES ON HER FOR SIX MONTHS! ♡

Chapter 50: The Most Important Thing to Me

HM?
BLINK
ARE YOU TWO GOING SOMEWHERE?

WE HAVE AN IMPORTANT MISSION!
AND WE DON'T KNOW WHEN WE'LL BE BACK, RIGHT?
HUH? KURO?
THAT'S RIGHT. WE DON'T KNOW.
KURO, WILL YOU STAY HERE?

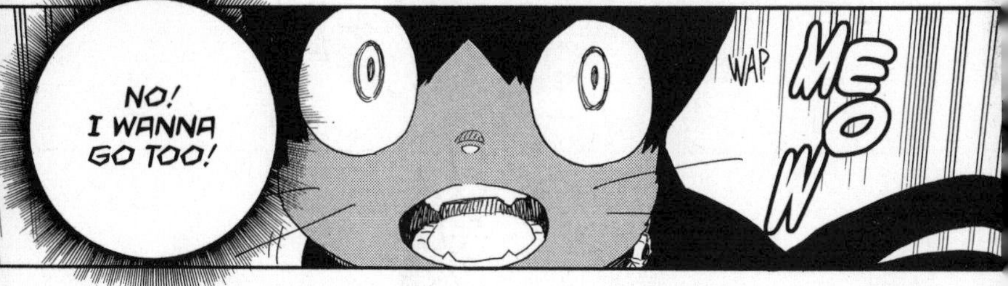
MEOW
WAP
NO! I WANNA GO TOO!

EVERYONE'S OUT?
OKAY, I UNDERSTAND.
YOU TOO, MOM.
I'LL CALL AGAIN.

BIP
...

I CAN'T DO ANYTHING TO HELP...
正十字学園駅
SEIJYUJI GAKUENEKI
CHATTER
CHATTER

*TRUE CROSS ACADEMY STATION

...BUT EVERYONE...

...PLEASE BE CAREFUL.

YEAH!

YOU CAN COUNT ON US!

SHIEMI!

!!

GASP

THIS IS MY CELL NUMBER. IF ANYTHING HAPPENS, CALL ME.

THANKS! OKAY, I'M GOING!

YOU'VE GOT TO RESCUE IZUMO.
SHIEMI!
THE TRAIN'S COMING! HURRY!
OH!
OKAY!

I KNOW WE'LL SAVE HER!
JUST WAIT FOR US!
CHATTER
CHATTER
PLEASE... BE SAFE!

NEAR INARI SHRINE IN SHIMANE PREFECTURE.
KLIK
THAT'S WHERE THEY ARE.
WE'RE GOING TO HANEDA AIRPORT TO CATCH A PLANE.
A PLANE?!
I'VE NEVER BEEN ON ONE!!
M-ME NEITHER...
KLIK

KLIK
I...I'M A LITTLE SCARED TO FLY...
CAN'T WE USE A MAGIC KEY?
KEYS CAN'T HANDLE THIS MANY PEOPLE.
Like when we went to Kyoto...
KLIK
HOW DID YOU KNOW THEY'RE IN SHIMANE?

KLIK
I SUMMONED A DOLL AND PLANTED IT ON IZUMO KAMIKI.
POK
POK
KLIK
I CAN LOCATE THE OBJECTS I SUMMON.
THEY'RE LIKE TRANSMITTERS.

KLIK

WHEN DID HE DO THAT?

KAMIKI AND PAKU ARE FROM INARI IN SHIMANE PREFECTURE.

OH, REALLY?

SO THEY KIDNAPPED HER AND TOOK HER BACK TO WHERE SHE CAME FROM?

Uh, where's Shimane?

KLAK

I WONDER WHY?

Terminal 2

VRRIII

LADIES AND GENTLEMEN, PREPARE FOR DEPARTURE. PLEASE MAKE SURE YOUR SEAT BELTS ARE FASTENED...

G...
GAAAH!
GWOOOSH
WE'RE FLYING!!
HEY! WE'RE FLYING, YUKIO!!
RATTLE
RIN, PIPE DOWN.
KLATTER
HEY, EVERYONE!
I MADE BOX LUNCHES! WANT ONE?
SHIEMI, WAIT UNTIL THE PLANE LEVELS OUT...

PING
SHF
WELL THEN...

...IT'S AN HOUR AND A HALF TO SHIMANE.
This is scary...
Here you go.
SO I'LL FILL YOU IN ON THE SITUATION.

LAST NIGHT, SERAPHIM FROM THE ILLUMINATI CONDUCTED SUICIDE BOMBINGS...
...ON THE HEADQUARTERS OF THE KNIGHTS OF THE TRUE CROSS AND ALL BRANCHES AND FIELD OFFICES.

IS THAT WHY I HAVEN'T BEEN ABLE TO CONTACT ANYONE IN MYODHA?
THE KYOTO OFFICE IS PROBABLY IN CHAOS BECAUSE OF THE ATTACKS.
I can't see...

THE EXTENT OF THE DAMAGE IS STILL UNCLEAR...
...BUT WE DO KNOW THE *GRIGORI* WERE INJURED TOO.
...!!

IT'S ON THE WEB. "ARE THE MYSTERIOUS EXPLOSIONS THE WORK OF TERRORISTS?!"
WELL, THAT'S NOT TOTALLY INCORRECT...

THE JAPAN BRANCH IS BUSY REPAIRING THE RUPTURED BARRIERS, EXTERMINATING THE DEMONS...
...AND DEALING WITH THE MASS MEDIA.

WHAT EXACTLY IS THE ILLUMINATI?

I'VE HEARD OF IT...
...BUT I NEVER THOUGHT IT ACTUALLY EXISTED.

THE ILLUMINATI IS A SECRET SOCIETY FOUNDED OVER 200 YEARS AGO.

IN MODERN TIMES, THEY PASSED OUT OF EXISTENCE.

BUT MANY STILL CLAIM TO BE ILLUMINATI.

THE ORDER MONITORS SECRET SOCIETIES AND OCCULTISTS AROUND THE WORLD...
...BUT IN THE LAST DOZEN YEARS OR SO...
...THE ILLUMINATI'S NAME HAS COME UP IN CONNECTION WITH INCIDENTS INVOLVING DEMONS.
THE ORDER HAS BEEN INVESTIGATING.
ZZZ ZZZ
IT'S HARD TO BELIEVE IT'S SUCH A MASSIVE TERROR ORGANIZATION.
A TERRORIST GROUP...
!
POP
BECAUSE OF THE CONTRACT OF MORINATH, I CAN'T SAY ANY MORE.
THAT'S ABOUT ALL I KNOW.

SHIMA...
...JOINED A GROUP LIKE THAT?
MNCH

SOME LEADER I AM!
GRIP

I DIDN'T UNDERSTAND A THING ABOUT HIM!
I THOUGHT I WAS WATCHING CLOSELY, BUT... I'M SO ASHAMED!
KONEKO-MARU...

AT LEAST, THAT'S WHAT I THOUGHT WHEN I SAW HIM LEAVE...
...WITH THAT SMILE ON HIS FACE...
...BUT...
...I...
SHIMA IS AN OLD FRIEND, SO I BELIEVE IN HIM!
I BELIEVE MY OWN EYES.
I CAN'T BE A TACTICIAN IF I DON'T HAVE FAITH IN MYSELF!!

TH... THAT'S RIGHT.

I THINK...
...WHAT YOU SAID IS RIGHT ON TARGET!
IT MUST BE TRUE!
THANK YOU, MORIYAMA.

WELL THEN...
...LET'S DIG INTO SHIEMI'S LUNCHES!
DON'T YOU WANT ANY, KURO?
UM...
...IT MAY NOT TASTE GOOD, BUT IT'S HEALTHY!
YOU'RE SO MODEST...
LET'S EAT!
CHO
MP
SPLOOEY!
IT... TASTES... GOOD...
TRMBL
TRMBL
HUH?!
IT TASTES LIKE GRASS!!!!
STOP TRYING TO BE COOL, YUKIO!
S-SORRY...
HOW CAN YOU EAT THAT, SUGURO?! IT'LL DESTROY YOUR TONGUE!

OKAY...

国内線 到着

Arrival

...UM...

国内線 到着

TA DUM

CAN I HELP YOU?

ARE YOU TOURISTS?

UM...

YES.

ALL THE BUSES AND TAXIS ARE OUT NOW.

IT WOULD BE FASTER TO WALK.

?!

FWSH
HUFF
HUFF
HUFF
WOW!
WHAT A PRETTY SEA OF RICE STALKS!
HUFF
HUFF
COOL! RICE FIELDS EVERY-WHERE!
THEY'RE HUGE!!
AND WE'RE *WALKING*...
I'LL GO ASK FOR DIRECTIONS.
ALL RIGHT.
SCRITCH

SUGURO...
...YOU'RE...
...TOO GLOOMY !!
BWAM
?!
FWUD
ROLL ROLL
HI-YAH!
CHEER UP, MAN!!
YOU CAN'T RESCUE ANYONE *THAT* WAY!!

R
R
...!!
R

B-BON!
RIN!!!!

?!
M
WHAT ARE THOSE TWO DOING?!

M
SHUT YOUR MOUTH...
M
I'M NOT LIKE YOU GUYS!!!!
YOU SURE DO...
...GET ANGRY FAST.

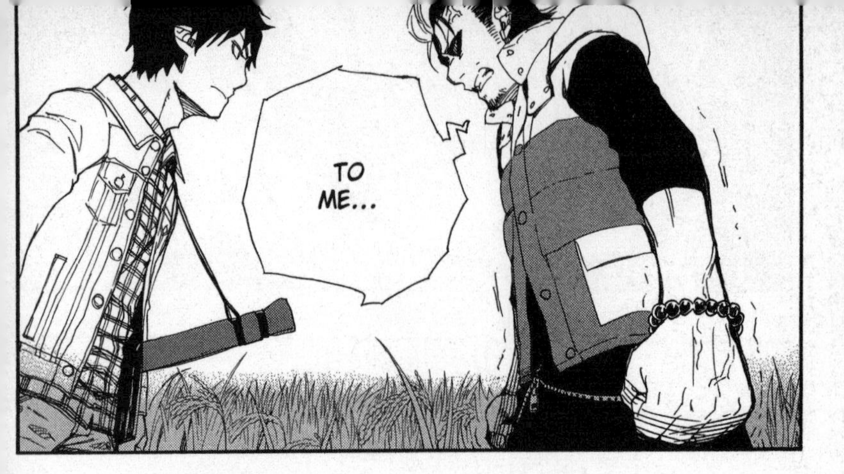
TO ME...

...HE'S *FAMILY!*

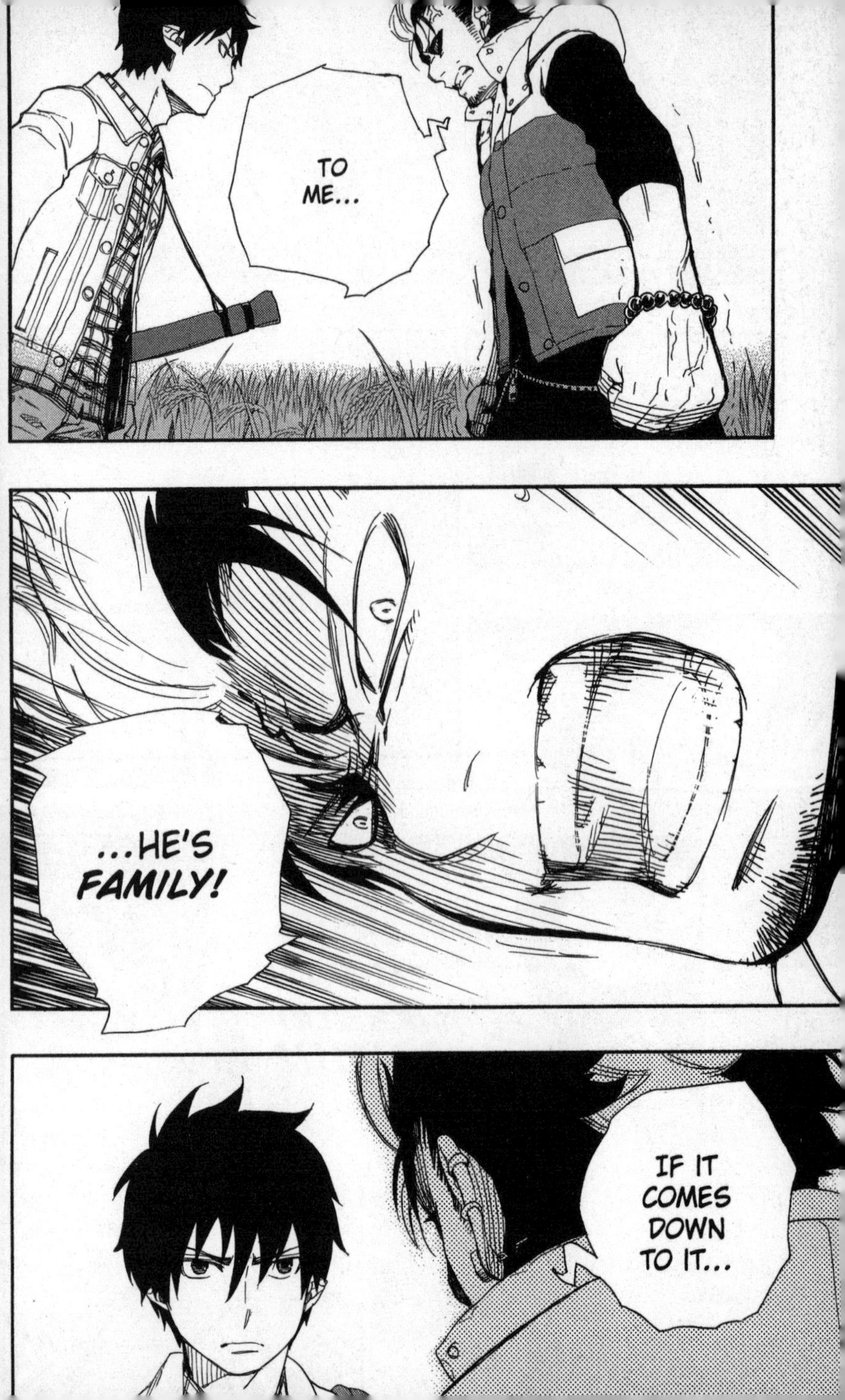

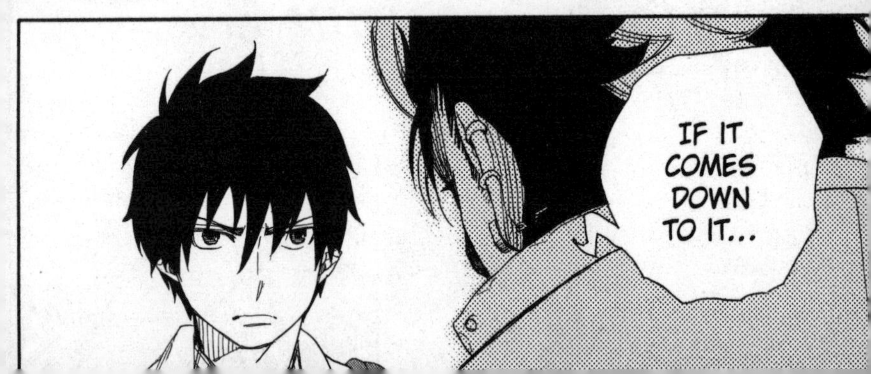
IF IT COMES DOWN TO IT...

I'LL KILL HIM...
...AND DIE MYSELF!!!!
BA
??!
HEY! I'M SERIOUS !!!!
BWAAA HAAA!! BWA HA HA!!!
M

THAT'S JUST LIKE YOU, SUGURO.
HUH?
I WAS THAT WAY TOO.
I WAS SAD BECAUSE I THOUGHT EVERYONE HATED ME.
BUT WHEN I THINK ABOUT IT NOW...
...YOU GUYS NEVER GAVE UP ON ME..

I'M GLAD SOMEONE'S ANGRY ABOUT IT.
SHIMA NEEDS SOMEONE LIKE THAT NOW.
SO DON'T CHANGE.
...
SKRE

YOU...
...REALLY...
HM?
HM?
YOU GONNA CRY?
...
DID I TOUCH A NERVE?
SWIP
SWIP
I'M SO EMBARRASSED!
GIMME A BREAK, DUMBASS!
WHAM
I'M GONNA RIP SHIMA LIMB FROM LIMB!!!!
HEEEY, SUGURO, DUDE! NOW THAT'S THE SPIRIT!
Shima may not appreciate it, but...
Whaddo I care?!
SHIMA REALLY IS GOING TO DIE...

*WELCOME TO INARI, INARI SHRINE 4 KM

HELP ME...

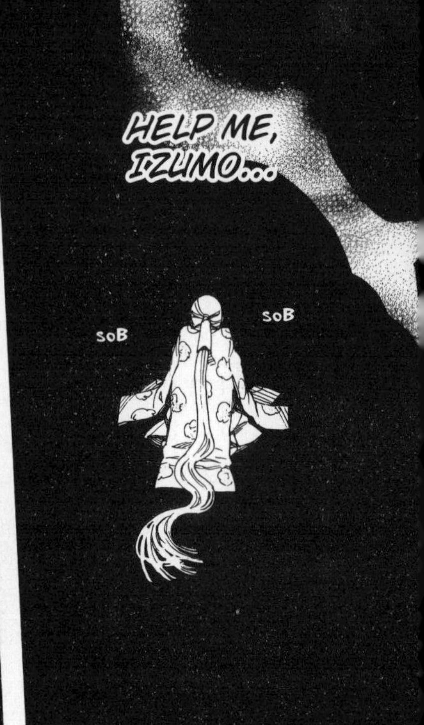
HELP ME, IZUMO...
SOB
SOB

I TRY SO HARD, SO WHY AM I NEVER HAPPY?

DON'T ASK ME.

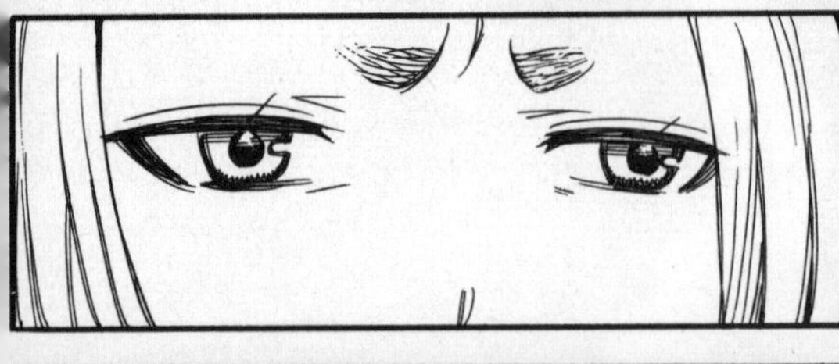

YOU'RE SO MEAN! YOU'RE MY DAUGHTER, BUT YOU WON'T HELP!
I'M THE UNHAPPIEST PERSON IN THE WORLD!

EVERYTHING...
I HATE YOU!
EVERY...
...SINGLE THING...
...IS YOUR FAULT!!
SIS...

TSUKUMO!
SIS...
ARE YOU CRYING?
NO...
TSUKUMO, YOU ARE SUCH A GOOD GIRL!
...I'M FINE.

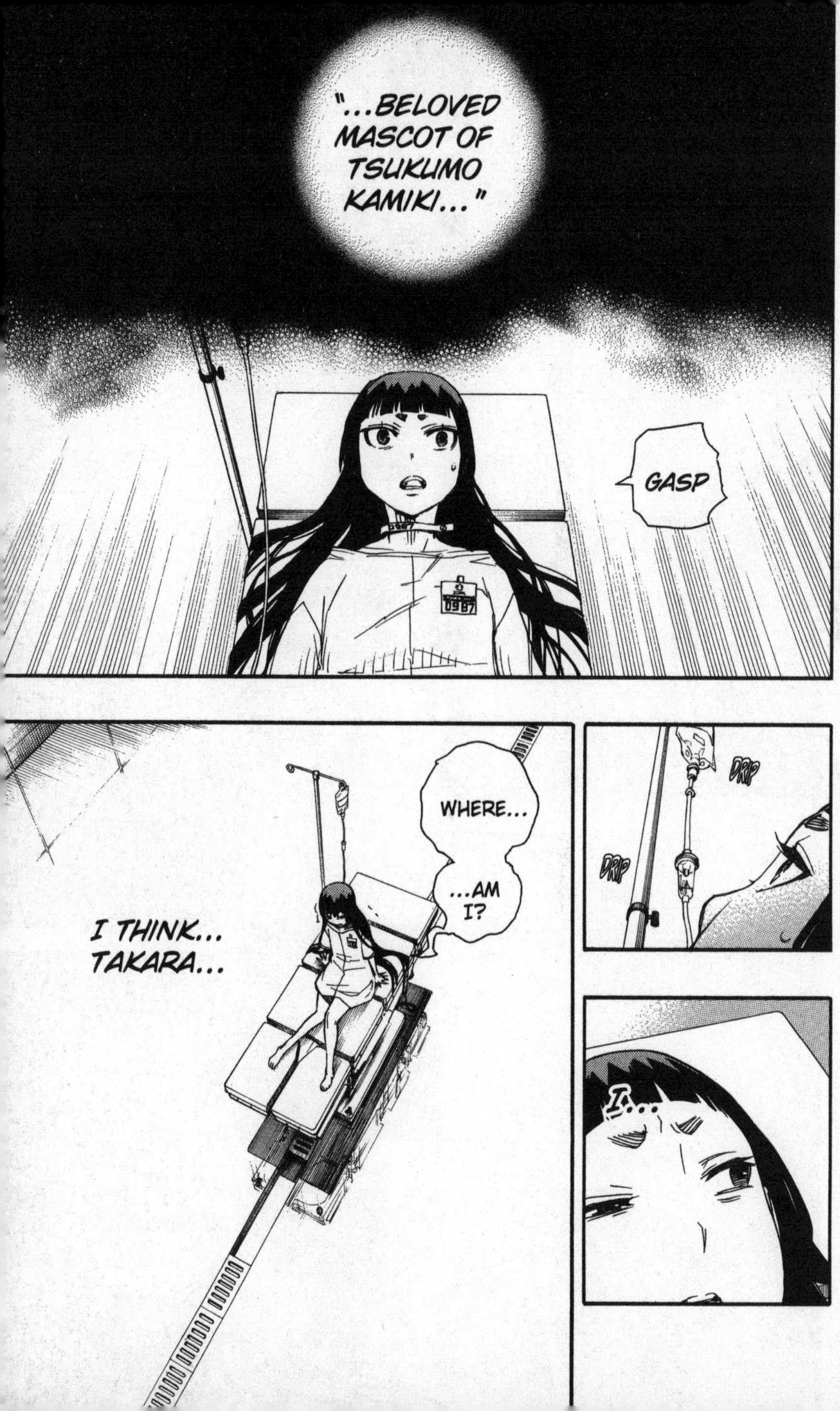

"...BELOVED MASCOT OF TSUKUMO KAMIKI..."

GASP

KACHAK

GAH

!!

HI, IZUMO! ♡

TNK

RENZO SHIMA...

I'M GLAD YOU'RE AWAKE.

YOU FEELING OKAY?

ARE YOU THIRSTY?

I DIDN'T CHANGE YOUR CLOTHES, SO DON'T WORRY ABOUT THAT.

PLOK

IT WAS ONE OF THE LADY RESEARCHERS.

I'VE BEEN ASLEEP TOO.

BUT, UM...
...THE HIGHER-UPS WANT TO TALK TO YOU.
CAN THEY COME IN NOW?
BA-BUMP
KLATAKATA
COME ON IN!

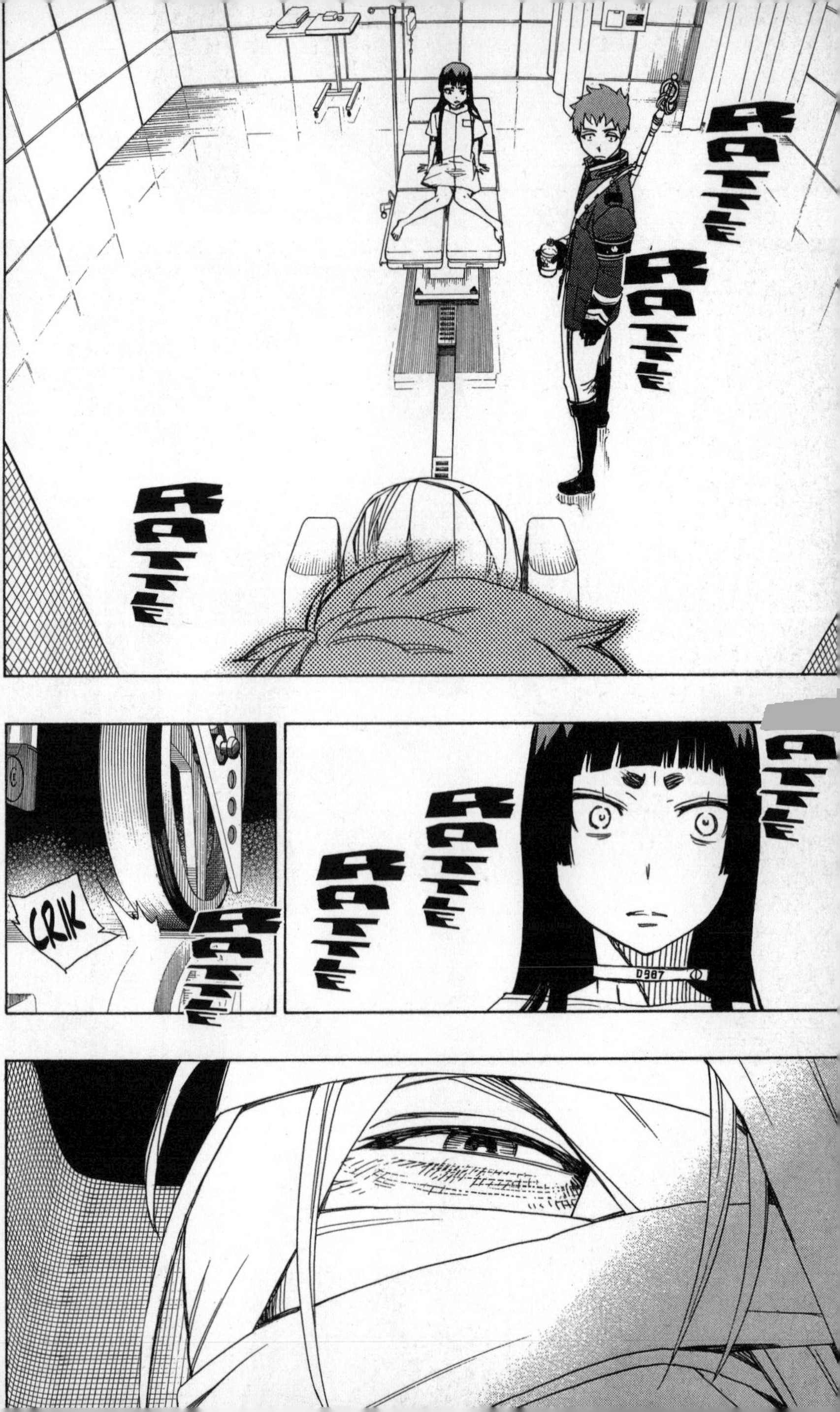

RATTLE
RATTLE
RATTLE

RATTLE
RATTLE
RATTLE

CRIK
RATTLE

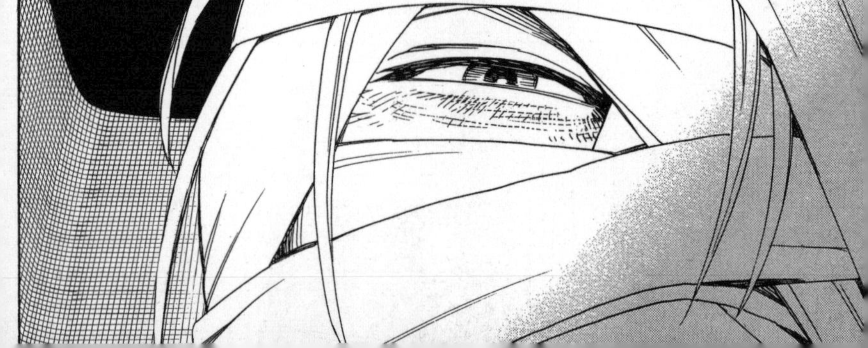

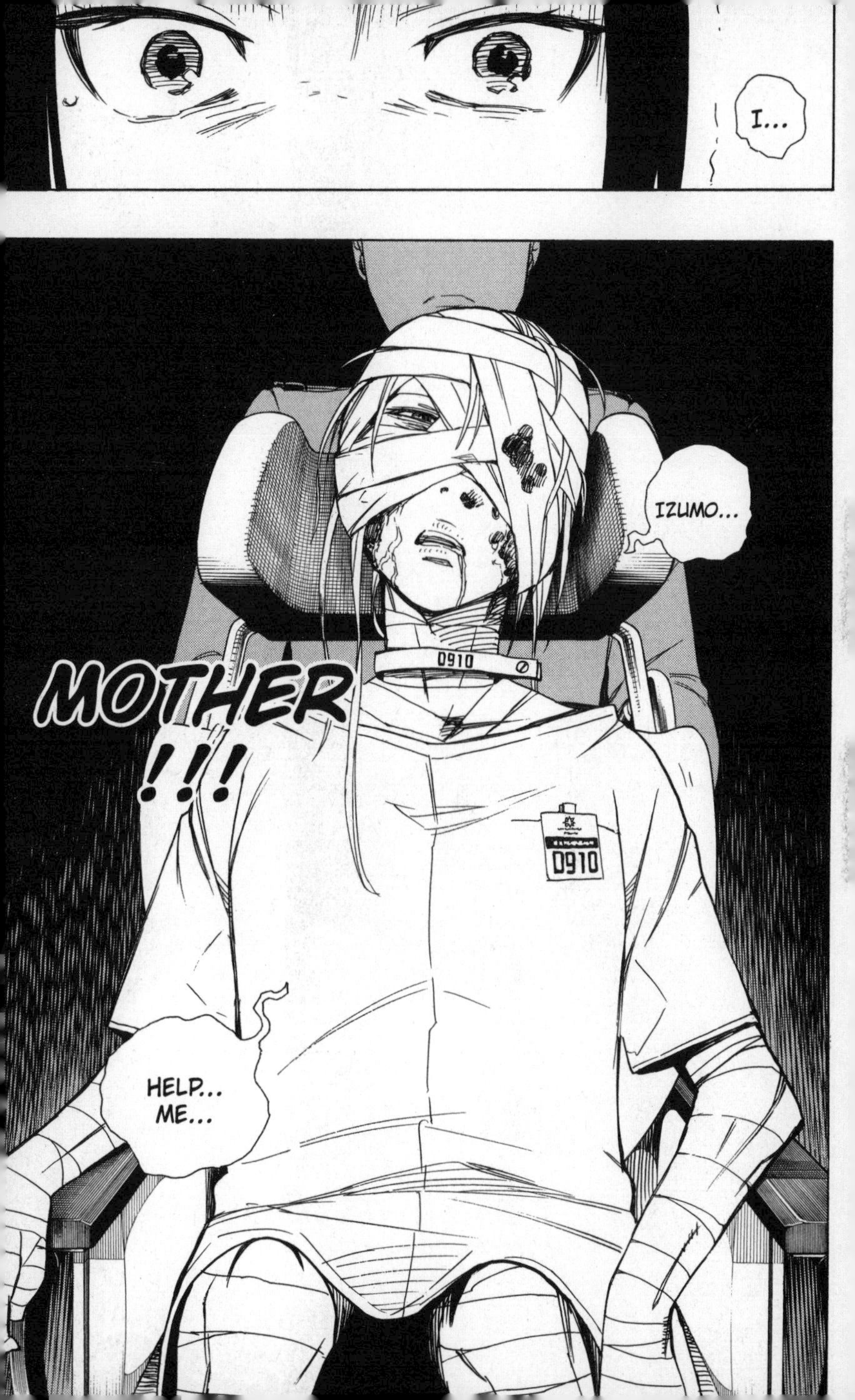

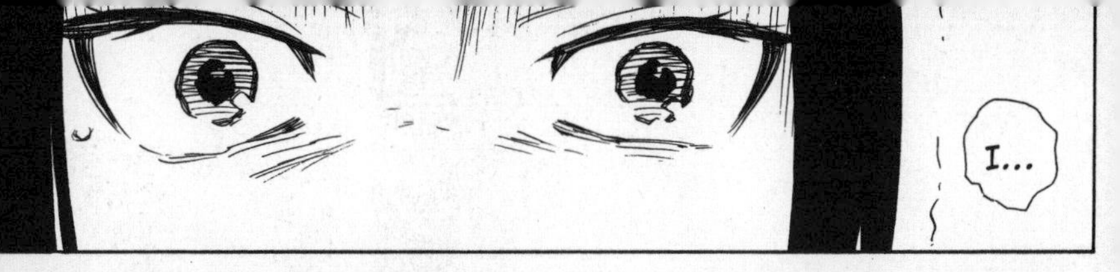

IZUMO...

0910

MOTHER!!!

0910

HELP... ME...

Blue Exorcist Chapter 50: The Most Important Thing to Me

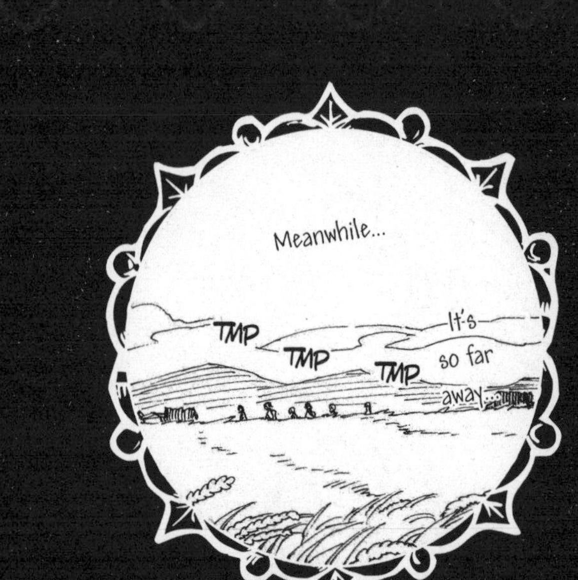
Meanwhile...
TMP
TMP
TMP
It's so far away...

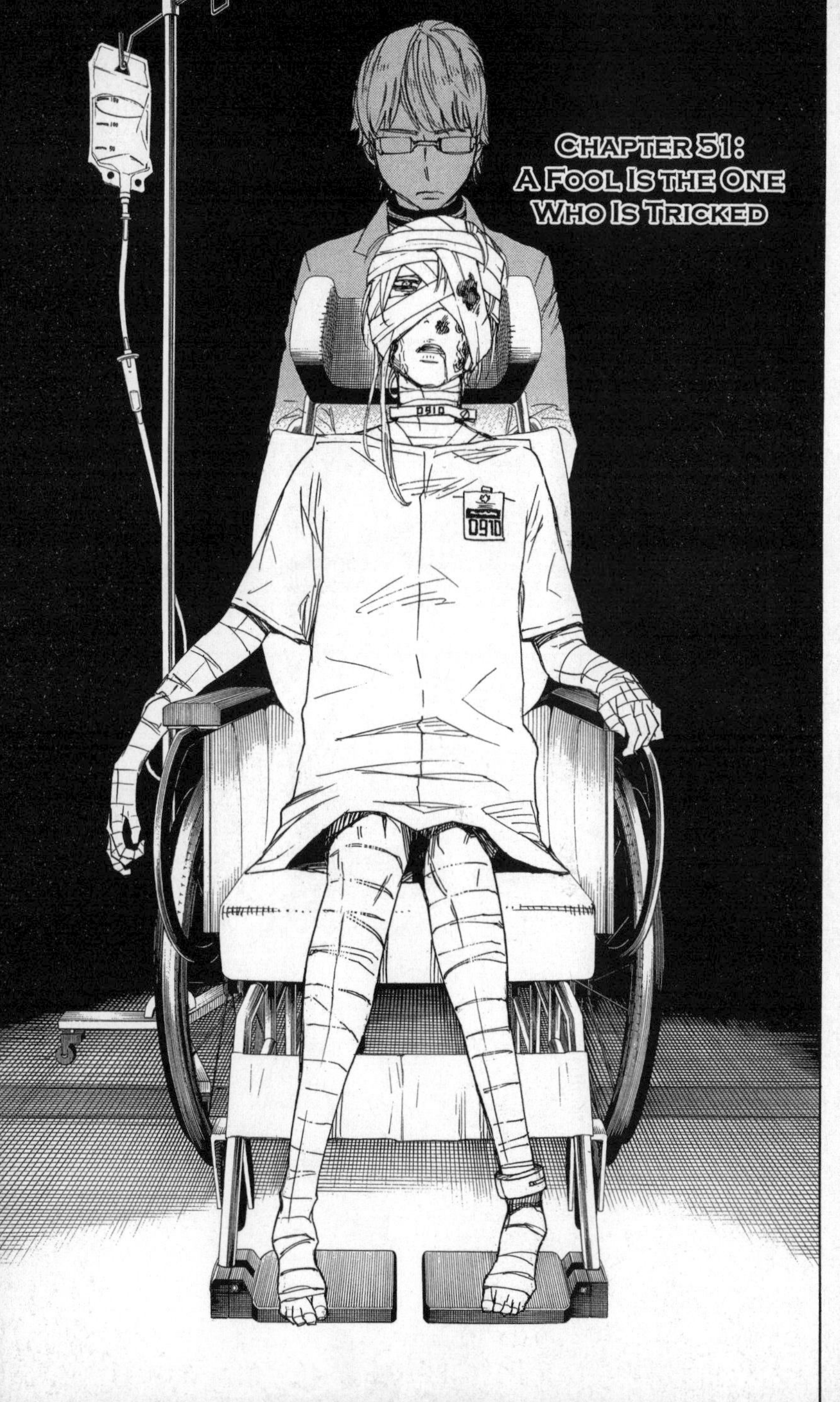
Chapter 51:
A Fool Is the One
Who Is Tricked
0910
0910

TWITCH
PLIP PLIP
SAVE...
...ME...
I...
...ZUMO...

M...

MOM...

NYAH HAH HAH HAH HAH!

AS YOU CAN SEE, THIS OLD HAG'S... OOPS! EXCUSE ME...

YOUR MOTHER'S BODY IS DETERIORATING FASTER THAN WE ANTICIPATED.

SHE IS OF NO FURTHER USE TO US. THAT'S WHY WE ASKED YOU TO COME HERE.
GRIN
GRIN
GRIN
YOU MONSTER!
I SAW THE RESULTS OF YOUR PHYSICAL EXAMINATION, BUT...
MM-HM... MM-HM...

STARE
YOU'VE FILLED OUT RATHER WELL. ♡
GRIN
THIS...
THIS ISN'T WHAT I WAS PROMISED!
TO BECOME AN EXORCIST, I NEED THE TITLE OF "TAMER SECOND CLASS," RIGHT?!
I *STILL* CAN'T INVOKE A SPIRIT!
OUR RESEARCH WILL TAKE CARE OF THAT.

GRIN
EVEN IF NOT OF THE SAME MATERIAL QUALITY...
...WE CAN FORCE A DEMON TO ***POSSESS*** YOU AND STAY WITH YOU. ♡
VOOO
THAT MAY HAVE BEEN THE PINNACLE OF YOUR MOTHER'S RESEARCH.
INDEED, IT MADE THE OLD HAG USEFUL TO THE WORLD AT THE VERY END.
PAT PAT
THOUGH IT'S ONLY BECAUSE ***I'M*** THE REAL GENIUS AROUND HERE.
IN ANY CASE...
IT MEANS THAT YOU DON'T HAVE TO WAIT ANY LONGER TO BECOME AN EXORCIST, IZUMO!

IN OTHER WORDS, *ANY* MEMBER OF THE KAMIKI FAMILY WILL DO.
SO WHAT'LL IT BE?
OR WILL YOU HAVE YOUR DEAR TSUKUMO DO IT INSTEAD?
STOP IT!
I'LL DO IT!
OH INDEED, YOU WILL!
NYAH HAH HAH HAH!
TSUKUMO'S TOO SMALL, AFTER ALL.
AND I PREFER A GIRL LIKE YOU ANYWAY, IZUMO.
NYAH HAH HAH!

TOMORROW, WE'LL CARRY OUT A THOROUGH EXAMINATION, AND IF THERE ARE NO PROBLEMS...
...WE'LL PUT YOU TO USE RIGHT AWAY, OKAY?
LICK
IZUMO. ♡
NYAH HAH HAH!
RATTLE
RATTLE
RATTLE
RATTLE
RATTLE
SAVE...
...ME...
...MO...
IZUMO, THERE'S A TALISMAN OVER THIS ROOM, SO I DON'T THINK YOU CAN SUMMON YOUR FAMILIARS.
SO JUST STAY QUIET, ALL RIGHT?
PSST
IF THE OLD MAN'S RESEARCH GOES WELL...
...I DON'T THINK ANY HARM WILL COME TO YOU.
SO, SEE YA.

GRAB

...ARE YOU SERIOUSLY JUST GOING TO LEAVE ME LIKE THIS?

UHH...
IS IT ALL RIGHT IF I STAY AWHILE?
WE'LL BE WATCHING.
WHIRRR

...GOT IT.

SO YOU'RE AWAKE.
MY WILD PRINCESS.

MEPHISTO...!

THE SERAPHIM'S EXPLOSION CAUGHT YOU HEAD ON.
THE LEFT SIDE OF YOUR ABDOMEN IN PARTICULAR WAS SEVERELY INJURED.
YOU SHOULD BE TAKING IT EASY IN THE HOSPITAL.
WHAT'S HAPPENING NOW...?!

UTTER CHAOS.

AS YOU CAN SEE, I'M BUSY RESURRECTING THE *BARRIER.*
WHAT ABOUT THE EXWIRES...?

I'VE SENT THEM AFTER IZUMO, WHO WAS TAKEN AWAY BY...
...THE ILLUMINATI, AND THE *SPY*, SHIMA.
WHAT?!
SEE? DIDN'T I TELL YOU...
SN
AP
SL
FSS...!!
UMP
SH-SHIMA?!
NOT TAKARA ...?!
Don't touch me, you clod!
TAKARA SPIES FOR *ME*. WHAT A SHAME.
OH, SPEAK OF THE DEVIL.
CHANGA CHANGA CHANGA CHANGA
POOF
MOE!

HELLO, HELLO? THIS IS MEPHISTO. ☆
WE'VE JUST ARRIVED AT OUR DESTINATION.

WHAT'S IT LIKE?

TURN
GOOD QUESTION. IT'S A GREAT BIG...

*BADGE: INARI FOX

WELCOME TO THE *INARI TAISHA SHRINE...*

...WHERE THE GOD OF THE HARVEST LIVES!

WHEN YOU COME TO THE INARI TAISHA SHRINE...

...MAKE SURE YOU STOP BY FOX ALLEY FIRST! YIP!

THEME PARK.
おきつね寿司
おいなりうどん

歓迎
歓迎
ようこそ
おきつね横町
稲生まんじゅう
草月庵
梅餡
稲生うどん
いなり餅
稲生ぜんざい
三月堂

HEH HEH HEH. TAKE A GOOD LOOK AROUND AND THEN REPORT BACK TO ME.
IF YOU RUN INTO ANY TROUBLE, JUST ASK TAKARA.
RIGHT THEN, GOOD LUCK, CAPTAIN OKUMURA!
BEEP
DON'T TELL ME...YOU SENT THE KIDS?!
WELL, WITH THE ADULTS IN SUCH A STATE...
YOU REALLY SHOULD BE TAKING IT EASY IN THE HOSPITAL TOO.
POFF
...!
YOU...!
YOU *KNEW* THIS WAS GOING TO HAPPEN, DIDN'T YOU...?
AND YOU KNOW WHAT'S GOING TO HAPPEN *NEXT* TOO...

SIR PHELES WANTS US TO SCOPE OUT THE AREA...
CHATTER
HM?!
WHERE'D TAKARA GO?
AS ALWAYS, BEFORE WE KNOW IT, HE'S GONE.
That jerk.
CHATTER
...OH, WELL. I GUESS WE'LL JUST HAVE TO ASK AROUND OURSELVES.
WELL, I'LL BE!

EVER SINCE I CAME HERE, I'VE FELT SO GOOD I COULDN'T HELP COMING BACK AGAIN!
OH, YOU TOO?
I'M HAVING SO MUCH FUN! I WISH I COULD STAY HERE FOREVER!
UM, EXCUSE ME.
IS THIS PLACE REALLY THAT GREAT?
IT'S OUR FIRST TIME HERE...

OH, YOUR FIRST TIME?
THIS PLACE WORSHIPS THE GOD OF FOOD, *TOYOKEBIME* AND OTHERS!
PRESS
YOU BOYS OUGHT TO VISIT HIS SHRINE RIGHT AWAY TOO!
IT WILL ENRICH YOUR LIFE!
PRESS
BUT NOT BEFORE YOU STROLL AROUND ***FOX ALLEY*** FIRST!
THE FOOD HERE IS ALL MADE USING LOCAL INGREDIENTS FROM SHIMANE, SO IT'S OUT OF THIS WORLD!!
ESPECIALLY THE INARI SOBA. DO YOURSELVES A FAVOR AND TRY SOME! I HIGHLY RECOMMEND IT!!
UH...
OKAY.
GRIN
GRIN
I UNDER-STAND.
GRIN
GRIN

歓迎
おきつね横町
THE SURROUNDING AREA'S QUIET AND SERENE, BUT...
...THIS PLACE IS PACKED WITH PEOPLE.
AND THEY'RE ALMOST ALL FOOD SHOPS!
AND IT'S LIKE THIS ALL THE WAY TO THE SHRINE.
So says the pamphlet.
IT'S THE INARI TAISHA SHRINE SPECIALTY, INARI SOBA!
IT'S DELICIOUS!
CARE FOR SOME MULTICOLORED INARI?
INARI ZENZAI!*
* SWEET RED-BEAN SOUP WITH PIECES OF RICE CAKE
AGONOYAKI !!*
WHOAAA, THAT SOUP SMELLS GOOD...!
I BET IT TASTES GREAT. LET'S HAVE A BITE.
SHIEMI'S GRASS SANDWICH WASN'T ENOUGH TO SATISFY MY STOMACH... OR MY TONGUE.
SNIFF
SNIFF
INDEED...
* A GRILLED TREAT MADE OF FISH PASTE PARTICULAR TO THE SHIMANE AREA.

IT'LL ALSO COUNT AS INVESTIGATING, SO LET'S EAT.
SCORE!!
WHOAA, LET'S DIG IN!!
BA DUM
SLURRP
YUUUUM!!
That was good!
AS GOOD AS THAT TASTED, IT'S NO WONDER THIS PLACE IS HOPPIN'.
Siiigh
THAT DOES IT! LET'S *INVESTIGATE* THE FOOD OVER THERE!!
HEY!
I'LL TAKE A LOOK AT THE SHRINE.
SHOULD WE COME WITH YOU TOO?
NO, KEEP AN EYE ON RIN FOR ME.

THIS PLACE IS QUIET IN COMPARISON.

PILLAR: INARI TAISHA

WHAT?

YOU'LL BE MOVING IN?

YEAH! I WAS CHOSEN! IT FEELS LIKE A DREAM...

I HEAR LESS THAN TWENTY PERCENT GET IN.

GOSH, I'M JEALOUS.

I'D HOPED TO GET IN TOO, BUT IT WAS A NO-GO FOR ME.

...?!

SO...
ALL WE'VE LEARNED IS THAT THE FOOD IN FOX ALLEY IS DELICIOUS, RIGHT?!
TMM TMM TMM
BDM BDM BDM
SPEAK FOR YOURSELF!
I GOT THE IMPRESSION THAT A LOT OF THE TOURISTS COME HERE AGAIN AND AGAIN.
SQUEAK SQUEAK
IT'S TRUE, THE CROWD AT THE SHRINE WAS PRETTY NORMAL.
AND IT'S THE FOOD, RATHER THAN THE SHRINE, THAT THEY'RE OBSESSED WITH.

I OVERHEARD A CONVERSATION ABOUT AN APARTMENT HOUSE CALLED "DREAM TOWN INARI."

I HEARD ABOUT IT TOO.

IT'S THAT PLACE RIGHT NEXT TO THE SHRINE.

WHAT IS *THAT?!*

BADUUUUUUM

SHRINE

DREAM TOWN INARI

IT SEEMS EVERYBODY WANTS TO GET IN THERE.

DO THEY WANT TO STAY HERE THAT BADLY?!
HOW FAR ARE THEY WILLING TO GO?!
ABOUT THAT...
THE SIGHTSEEING MAP THEY PROVIDE AT THE INFORMATION DESK...

Access Guide
Published by the Inari Light Foundation
...SAYS IT'S THE "INARI LIGHT FOUNDATION"!
DOESN'T THAT NAME REMIND YOU OF THE ILLUMINATI?

...! YOU DON'T MEAN...
IF THERE'S SOMETHING WE DON'T KNOW, WE SHOULD JUST ASK THE LOCALS.

TAKARA!!
WHERE HAVE YOU BEEN ALL THIS TIME?
BLOOP
IT TOOK A WHILE TO FIND A DOLL THAT WAS GOOD ENOUGH.

HE COST 1.2 MILLION YEN SO DEDUCT THAT FROM THE ORDER'S EXPENSES.
Here's the receipt.
FWIP
Million ?!
WHAT?!

HOOO

"TO UKANO MITAMANOKAMI..."
"...I FEARFULLY DREADFULLY DECREE..."
"PRESENT TO US ONE WHO IS CONNECTED TO IZUMO KAMIKI AND THIS LAND."
!!
SHHH
SS
HE'S SUMMONING IT INTO THE DOLL!
SO HE HAS THE POWER OF A TAMER?!
FLASH
SO YOU'RE IZUMO KAMIKI'S FAMILIAR!
INDEED, I AM A SERVANT OF UKANO MITAMA-NOKAMI!
PLOK
PLOK PLOK
TELL US EVERYTHING ABOUT IZUMO KAMIKI AND THIS LAND!
I AM OF THE 8TH RANK THE FOX GOD MIKE!

YOU DARE CLAIM THAT I'M THE FAMILIAR OF AN INEXPERIENCED LITTLE GIRL LIKE HER?!
PLEASE CEASE YOUR JOKING!
FIRST AND FOREMOST, WHAT CONNECTION DO YOU HAVE TO HER?!

IZUMO IS OUR FRIEND.
!

OUR ENEMY IS IN THIS AREA. HOW IS IZUMO KAMIKI CONNECTED?
WILL YOU SPEAK OR STAY SILENT?
IF YOU DON'T WANT THIS, THEN WE'LL ASK ANOTHER.
VERY WELL.

I WILL TELL YOU ABOUT THIS LAND AND THAT GIRL.

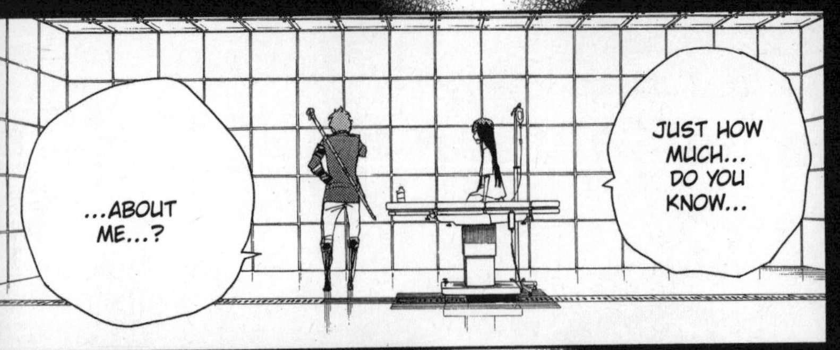

JUST HOW MUCH... DO YOU KNOW...
...ABOUT ME...?

WHY, NOTHING AT ALL!

AT FIRST THEY ONLY SHOWED ME A PHOTO OF A GIRL THEY SAID WAS OF GREAT IMPORTANCE TO THE SOCIETY.

AND YOU'RE SUCH A CUTIE, IZUMO, I ENJOYED OBSERVING YOU.

...WAIT A SECOND...

HOW LONG HAVE YOU BEEN WITH THE ILLUMINATI?!

UM...

SINCE RIGHT BEFORE ENROLLING AT TRUE CROSS ACADEMY?

TODO TALKED TO ME AND...

...SAID THAT SINCE I'D BE GOING TO THAT SCHOOL, I SHOULD KEEP AN EYE ON YOU AND THE OTHER CRAM SCHOOL STUDENTS...

...AND REPORT TO HIM IF ANYTHING CAME UP. THAT'S ALL, SEE?

...!!

WHEN THAT WHOLE THING WITH THE IMPURE KING WENT DOWN, I WAS NERVOUS INSIDE.

BUT I TOOK A HANDS-OFF POLICY WITH THAT AND WAS TOLD TO JUST PLAY MY PART.

BECAUSE I HATE THEM ALL!

Snort!

BON AND KONEKOMARU ...
MY OLDER BROTHERS, MY FAMILY AND THE MYODHA. THEY'RE ALL JUST A PAIN IN THE ASS.
I WISH I COULD JUST THROW THEM ALL AWAY.

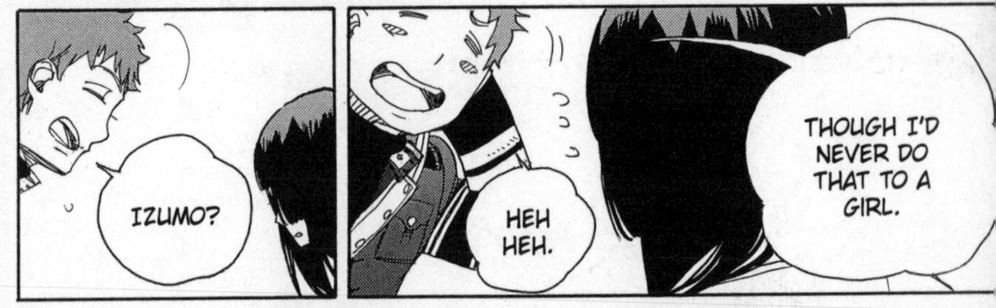

THOUGH I'D NEVER DO THAT TO A GIRL.
HEH HEH.
IZUMO?

SLAP
I KNOW THAT A *FOOL* IS THE ONE WHO IS TRICKED.
BUT...
I...
...THOUGHT YOU GUYS...

...WERE FRIENDS!
0987
YOU TRAITOR!!
HMPH.

YOU'RE MAD?!
Ha ha!
THAT'S A SURPRISE!
I THOUGHT YOU AND I WERE TWO OF A KIND, IZUMO.
OH.
I ALMOST FORGOT.
HERE!
THIS WAS INSIDE THE MAID OUTFIT YOU WERE WEARING, IZUMO. I'VE BEEN HOLDING ON TO IT.
IT'S A GOOD LUCK CHARM, RIGHT?
HERE.
THAT'S RIGHT.

IT'S JUST LIKE YOU SAID, PINK HEAD.

RR RR

MBLE

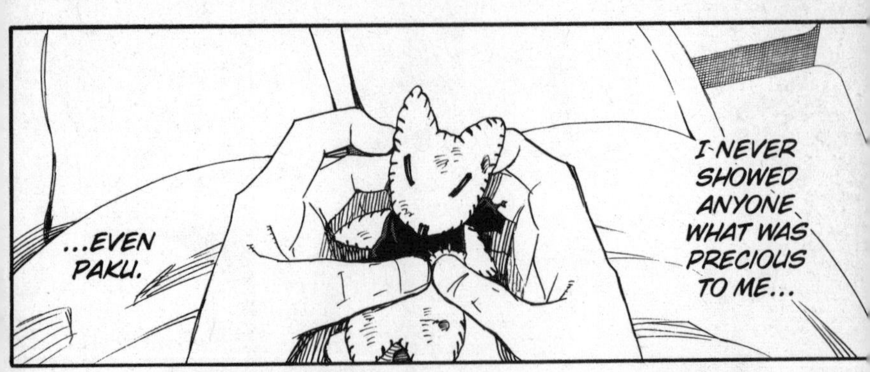

I NEVER SHOWED ANYONE WHAT WAS PRECIOUS TO ME...
...EVEN PAKU.

BECAUSE I DON'T TRUST ANYONE.

I'M THE TRAITOR AROUND HERE...!

0987

WHAT ARE YOU DOING? FEELING HOMESICK?

!!

FLASH

KLIK

Heh heh...

...

AS IF.

WE NEEDN'T GO THAT FAR BACK IN TIME.
IT ALL STARTED A FEW YEARS AGO...!

UNTIL FIVE SHORT YEARS AGO...

...THIS LAND OF INARI WAS PURE!

I WILL NOW TELL YOU OF IZUMO, THE 11-YEAR-OLD DAUGHTER OF THE KAMIKI FAMILY...
...AND THIS LAND.

Blue Exorcist Chapter 51: A Fool Is the One Who Is Tricked

Chapter 52:
I Can't Rely on Anyone
THE MAIN DEITY OF INARI TAISHA SHRINE...
...IS TOYOUKEBIME, WHO PRESIDES OVER PROSPEROUS CROPS...
...AND HAS PROTECTED THE LANDS OF INARI SINCE ANCIENT TIMES.

THE INAMI FAMILY, WHOSE ANCESTORS WERE DIVINE SERVANTS OF UKANO MITAMANOKAMI, ADMINISTERED THE RITES.
THE KAMIKI FAMILY IS A BRANCH OF THAT LINEAGE.
THEY ARE A CLAN THAT HAS MIXED WITH FOX GODS AND GAINED DIVINE POWER...
...SIMILAR TO THAT BOY WHO CLOAKS HIMSELF IN GODLY FLAME.
!
YOU WOULD SAY THEY HAVE THE BLOOD OF *DEMONS*.

COME TO THINK OF IT...
MAYBE YOU DON'T KNOW...
...BUT THERE ARE TONS OF PEOPLE WITH DEMON BLOOD.

OVER TIME...
A family stretching back over 1,000 years...
...THE MAIN BLOODLINE HAS WEAKENED SO NOW THEY ARE LITTLE DIFFERENT FROM ORDINARY FOLK.

HOWEVER, IN ORDER TO FULFILL THEIR *DUTY*...

...THE KAMIKI FAMILY HAS LONG MAINTAINED THE POWER IN ITS BLOOD.

Chapter 52: I Can't Rely on Anyone

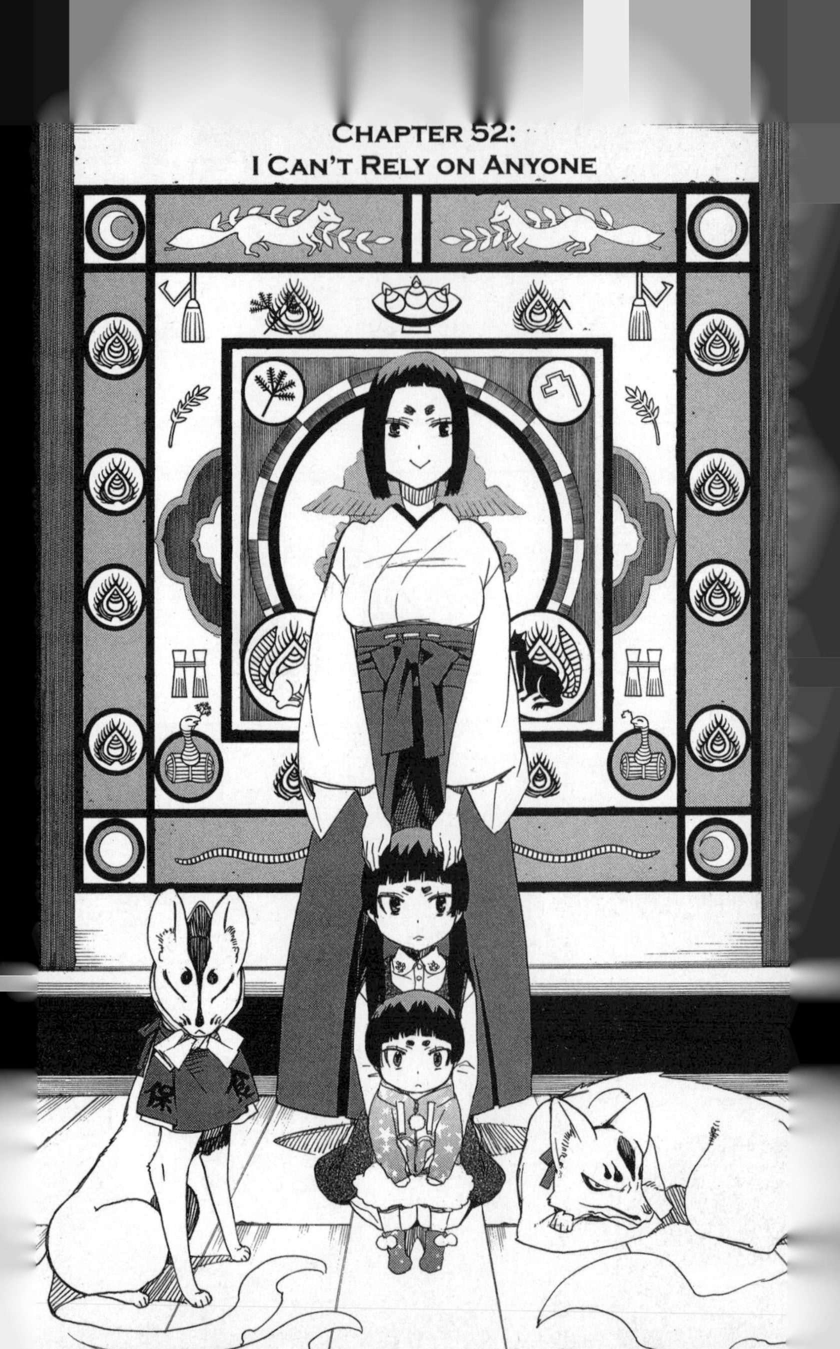

THE KAMIKI FAMILY HAS REMAINED NEAR THE GREAT SHRINE AND PROTECTED IT.
CHIRP
CHIRP
CHIRP
IZUMO KAMIKI WAS BORN HERE.
CLINK
TINK
HER MOTHER IS THE FAMILY'S SIXTY-FOURTH HEAD PRIESTESS.

SOB
TAMAMO KAMIKI.
WAAAH!! HELP ME, IZUMO-OO!
SOB
EVERY-ONE...
...ACTS SO COLD TOWARD MEEE!!
SNIFF
WAAAH!
THEY ACT LIKE IT'S ALL MY FAULT!!
OF COURSE THEY DO.
SOCIETY FROWNS ON WHAT YOU'RE DOING.
GRND
GRND
GRND
BUT IT'S NOT WRONG! SOJI AND I ARE IN LOVE!
GLEAM GLEAM
URGH URGH URGH
THERE'S NOTHING TO BE ASHAMED OF!

JEEZ.
PULL YOURSELF TOGETHER!!
MOMS DON'T USUALLY NEED THEIR DAUGHTER'S HELP!!
GRAH
WHAT?! YOU'RE SO COLD!
YOU'RE MY DAUGHTER, SO YOU HAVE TO HELP ME!!
...!!
BESIDES, SOJI IS YOUR FATHER! SO TAKE THIS SERIOUSLY!
HA
HE'S NEVER COME TO SEE US EVEN ONCE!
IT'S LIKE WE DON'T HAVE A FATHER!
HE'S BUSY WITH HIS DUTIES!
HERE'S YOUR BREAKFAST, TAMA.
TNK
THANK YOU, UKE!
SOMEDAY WE'LL ALL BE TOGETHER AS A FAMILY...
TAMAMO, I HUNG THE WASH OUT TO DRY.
...AND I'LL BE A WONDERFUL MOTHER!!
THANK YOU,

CHATTER
CHATTER
BUT YOU LEAVE ALL THE HOUSEWORK TO THE FOX GODS!
That's being a "wonderful mother"?!
OH, THAT'S ALL RIGHT!
AFTER ALL, IT'S PART OF MY ABILITY!
RIGHT...
...GUYS?
YEAH!
YOU'RE OUR IDOL!!
HUMANOID FORM IS TIRING, BUT...
...YOU'RE SO CUTE THAT WE DON'T MIND!
VERY POPULAR
DON'T CODDLE HER!!
AS YOU CAN SEE...
...TAMAMO WAS AN IRRESPONSIBLE AND CARELESS WOMAN...
FORGET ABOUT THAT AND EAT!
YOU HAVE YOUR DUTY THIS MORNING!

OKAY!
...BUT AS PRIESTESS, SHE POSSESSED GREAT DIVINE POWER.
THE KAMIKI FAMILY'S DUTY WAS CONTAINING EVIL.

THE KILLING STONE...
...A DEMONIC STONE THAT SLAYS THE LIVING WHO APPROACH IT AND REJUVENATES THE DEAD.
IT IS THE ESSENCE OF THE FOX WITH A WHITE FACE, GOLDEN FUR AND NINE TAILS...
...THAT AN ONMYOJI ONCE DESTROYED.
THE KAMIKI FAMILY SEPARATED FROM THE INAMI TO SUBDUE THE CURSE OF NINE TAILS...
...AND ESTABLISHED THEIR BLOODLINE FROM THE AFOREMENTIONED ONMYOJI.

GENERATIONS OF SHRINE MAIDENS WHO WOULD BE CHIEF PRIESTESS TOOK THE NAME "TAMAMO"...
...AND DANCED THE SACRED DANCE OF SPIRIT INVOCATION.
THEY QUELLED NINE TAILS BY ASSIMILATING THE GODDESS AND BECOMING HER.
IZUMO'S MOTHER WAS THE STRONGEST MEDIUM EVER!

TAMAMO WAS AN UNUSUAL WOMAN...

...BUT SHE WAS DIFFICULT TO DISLIKE.

IZUMO AND TSUKUMO WERE THE ILLEGITIMATE CHILDREN OF SOJI INAMI, THE CHIEF PRIEST OF THE MAIN FAMILY.
PLEASE TAKE CARE OF TSUKUMO TODAY.
THEY GREW UP IN COMPLICATED CIRCUMSTANCES.

*SIGN: PRAYER HALL

SURE...
...I'LL TAKE HER.
GO ON IN, TSUKUMO.
AND SINCE SHE WAS FROM THE FAMILY THAT HANDLED THE KILLING STONE...
WHAT'S THE MATTER, TSUKUMO?
...PEOPLE LOOKED AT HER ASKANCE AND SNEERED AT HER.

I DON'T WANNA GO!
GRIP
IT'S ALL RIGHT.
WHERE'S THE GOOD-LUCK CHARM I GAVE YOU?
HERE!
AS LONG AS YOU HAVE THIS, YOU'RE NOT ALONE! YOU'RE STRONG!

OKAY, PUT IT BACK INSIDE YOUR BEAR.
I'LL COME BACK AFTER SCHOOL.
OKAY...

SIGH

SHE COULDN'T EVEN RELAX OUTSIDE THE SHRINE.
I HOPE...
...THEY DON'T TREAT TSUKUMO COLDLY.
MY KIN ARE WATCHING OVER HER, SO SHE'LL BE FINE.
YEAH, BUT...
...WOULD YOU GO CHECK ON HER?
WELL, IF I *HAVE* TO!
WHS
H
LOOK! KAMIKI'S TALKING TO HERSELF AGAIN!
TEE HEE HEE!
SPOOKY!
SHE'S GIVING OFF THAT SUPERNATURAL VIBE!
MY MOM SAYS...
...THAT KAMIKI'S *ODDNESS* COMES FROM HER FAMILY.
HA HA HA HA!
THEN WE SHOULDN'T LAUGH.
HA HA HA!
SOME PEOPLE LAUGH AT ANYONE WHO ISN'T LIKE THEM.
IZUMO WAS ALWAYS ALONE.

YAAY! ♪
YAAY! ♪
YOU CAN DO IT!
GOOD JOB!
WHSH
THERE'S NO CHOICE.
I CAN'T RELY ON ANYONE.

I'VE GOT TO BE STRONG!
TMP
TWIST
OW!
FWUD
ROLL ROLL ROLL
UGH!
CLUMSY DUNCE!
TRYING TO COPY TAMAMO'S INVOCATION?
YOU'RE NOT EVEN CLOSE!
WHAT ?!
N-NO... YOU DON'T UNDER-STAND!!
BLUSH
I...I JUST THOUGHT THAT I SHOULD...
...LEARN IT SOON!

EVEN IF YOU LEARN IT AND TAKE OVER FROM TAMAMO...
...WE'LL NEVER SERVE YOU!
YOU'RE NOT EVEN CUTE!
NOT CUTE AT ALL!
WHAT?!
IS CUTENESS A REQUIREMENT ?!
HA HA!
INARI TAISHA HAS FOXES EVERYWHERE!
PLEASED TO MEET YOU...
...IZUMO KAMIKI! ♡ HA HA HA!!
...?!
PROFESSOR GEDOIN...
...ALLOW ME TO HANDLE THIS.
TCH! BECAUSE A WOMAN IS LESS THREATENING?

SORRY TO BOTHER YOU.
TAK
WE ARE RESEARCHERS FOR THE CUTTING-EDGE DEMON RESEARCH INSTITUTE KNOWN AS THE *ILLUMINATI.*
DEMONS ?!
ILLU... MI...??
YES.
WE USE THE WORD "DEMON" TO DESCRIBE BEINGS THAT OTHERS CANNOT SEE.
LIKE THOSE FOXES OVER THERE.

WHO ARE YOU CALLING A DEMON?!
Y...
YOU CAN SEE THEM?!
YES.
I'M GLAD WE BUMPED INTO YOU.
WE HAVE COME TO ASK SOME QUESTIONS...

...ABOUT THE KILLING STONE IN YOUR FAMILY'S CARE.
!
WE IN THE ILLUMINATI ARE WORKING TO CLOSE THE DISTANCE BETWEEN HUMAN AND DEMON.
IF WE CAN DRAW OUT THE POWER OF NINE TAILS FROM THE STONE...
...WE CAN USHER IN A WORLD WHERE DEMON AND HUMAN LIVE AS ONE.
DO YOU MIND IF WE TALK TO YOU?
...

THAT SOUNDS FISHY TO ME!
NO ONE BUT A KAMIKI CAN TOUCH THE STONE!
AND I CAN'T BELIEVE YOU WANT TO BRING OUT NINE TAILS!
GOOD-BYE!
IT DOESN'T HAVE TO BE RIGHT NOW.
WAIT!
WE STUDY DEMONS, SO IF YOU HAVE ANY TROUBLE, CALL ME.
I SUFFERED AS A CHILD BECAUSE I COULD SEE DEMONS...
...SO I MIGHT BE ABLE TO HELP.
...!

I L
吉田ーマリア
MARIA YOSHIDA
I'M HOME!
MOM! SOME WEIRD PEOPLE WERE JUST-
WAAAH!! IZUMO! I'VE GOT A DATE!!
I'M GONNA SEE SOJI AGAIN! I'M SO HAPPY!!
WATCH TSUKUMO FOR ME!!
RUB RUB
SEE YOU- OOF!
KYA HA HA
MM-MM!
YOU'RE MY TREASURES! BYE!
BANG
A BUSINESS CARD!!
...
WANT IT? I'LL GIVE IT TO YOU!
THANKS!
I HAVE A BUSINESS CARD TOO.
I'LL GIVE YOU ONE!
I made them myself!

THAT WAS HOW THEY GRADUALLY MOVED INTO THIS PLACE.
THE INARI TOURISM AND URBANIZATION PROJECT??
WHAT'S THAT?
IT'S A PLAN...
...TO ATTRACT MORE TOURISTS AND PILGRIMS TO THE SHRINE AREA.
THE DEVELOPMENT FUNDS WILL COME FROM THE *INARI ENLIGHTENMENT FOUNDATION.*
IT COULD REALLY LIVEN UP THE SHRINE!
OH! I DON'T REALLY GET IT...
...BUT IF YOU LIKE IT, THEN I DO TOO. ♡
HEY, UH... SOJI? ♡
HUG
COME VISIT MY HOUSE SOMETIME!
THE CHILDREN WANT TO SEE YOU! ♡

WELL TAMAMO, I'VE BEEN MEANING...

...TO SPEAK WITH YOU ABOUT THAT.

WAP

YES, HONEY? ♡

DON'T TRY TO GET ME AND THE CHILDREN TOGETHER.

I DON'T ***WANT*** TO SEE THEM.

I LIKE YOU, BUT IF YOU KEEP SAYING THAT...

...I WON'T WANT TO SEE ***YOU*** EITHER.

AFTER THAT, TAMAMO WAS NO LONGER HERSELF.

TAMAMO?

YOU SHOULD REST, TAMA.

IF YOU INVOKE IN YOUR CURRENT STATE...

YEAH!

...NINE TAILS WILL GET THE BETTER OF YOU!

I'M FINE.

BUT SOON AFTER, SHE BEGAN NEGLECTING HER DUTIES.

EACH DAY, SHE SECLUDED HERSELF WITH THE INAMI HEAD PRIEST.

YOU'RE GOING OUT TOO MUCH!

TSUKUMO'S LONELY!

SHUT UP!

IT'S ALL BECAUSE OF YOU TWO!!

BEFORE LONG...

...SHE DIDN'T COME HOME AT ALL.
HEY, SIS?
WHEN WILL TAMA COME HOME?
WHEN SHE FINISHES WORK.
SHE'S BUSY.
OH...
AFTER I PUT YOU TO BED...
...I'M GOING TO BRING MOTHER BACK!
WEEOO
WEEOOO

WEEOO

WEEOOO

SKRK

CHATTER

CHATTER

CHATTER

?!

UM, DID SOMETHING HAPPEN?
THE WHOLE INAMI HOUSEHOLD COLLAPSED!
THEY'RE ALL UNCONSCIOUS!
BUT THE CHIEF PRIEST AND TAMAMO...
...WON'T COME OUT!
I SHOULDN'T SAY THIS...
SIS...?
...BUT YOUR MOTHER IS HORRIBLE!
MAYBE SHE...
HEAD PRIES OPEN T DOOR
WHAM
WHAM
WHAM
WE'LL HAVE TO FORCE OUR WAY IN!
HEAD PRIEST
HEE HEE...

HEE HEE HEE... MY DEAR... DEAR... DEAR...
...SOJI...
WHA...
WHAT'S GOING ON HERE?!
!!
HEAD PRIEST! OH NO!
M-MISTRESS TAMAMO!
IS SHE POSSESSED?!

BEFORE ANYONE NOTICED, IT WAS TOO LATE.
Z Z Z Z Z
GRAAAH
...?!
KRASH
JOLT

WHAM
WHUD
CRASH
SMACK
CLATTER CLATTER
WHAT'S GOING ON...?
RATTLE
GASP
BLOOD!
HUFF
CHOMP SPLURT
HUFF HUFF

...
MOM?
IZUMO...
...ARE YOU GOING TO INTERFERE WITH ME AGAIN?
EVERYTHING... EVERY... SINGLE... THING...
...IS YOUR FAULT!!
BECAUSE OF YOU TWO, I COULDN'T HAVE SOJI!!

I WISH YOU'D NEVER BEEN BORN!
IF IT WEREN'T FOR YOU TWO...
BAM
SMASH
KRAK
SWSH
KRAK
EEK... KYAAH!

!!
MM...
...MM...
S...
STOP!
DWSH
DAMNED DIVINE SERVANTS!
SWSH
TAMAMO!!
BA
BAM

SAY IT ISN'T TRUE!!
TOMP
UKE!
MIKE!!
THP
TAMA IS LOST!!
SHE HAS COMPLETELY ASSIMILATED NINE TAILS!
RUN!!
GAH!!
THUD
MIKE!!
AH HA HA HA HA HA HA HA!!
HAAA HA HA HA HA!!

MOM...
MOM...
HUFF
HUFF
MOM !!!!
TRIP
AGH!
UNGH...
OUCH...
SORRY, TSUKUMO!!
IF YOU HAVE ANY TROUBLE, CALL ME.
I L
吉田・マリア
MARIA YOSHIDA

RRRING
RRRING
CLIK
HELLO?
THIS IS IZUMO KAMIKI!
NINE TAILS HAS POSSESSED MY MOTHER!
WHAT?
IZUMO?! WHAT DO YOU NEED?
GET NINE TAILS OUT OF MY MOTHER!!
BLUE EXORCIST 12 - END -

BLUE EXORCIST CHAPTER 52: I CAN'T RELY ON ANYONE

BONUS

An Illustrated Guide to Demons

FILE 31

Samael

High Level

King of Time. Excluding Satan, who reigns as a god, Samael is the second highest authority in Gehenna. He governs demons associated with time and space. He has countless names in different eras, countries and places. Some lands worship him like a god.

At present, he possesses the body of a human male and as Johann Faust the Fifth, has established a position of some status. He is enjoying his life in Assiah to the fullest.

Lucifer

High Level

King of Light. Excluding Satan, who reigns as a god, he is the highest authority in Gehenna. He governs demons associated with light. He has countless names depending on era, country and place. Some lands worship him like a god.

At present, he possesses the body of a human male and leads a secret society known as the Illuminati.

The Impure Princess

High Level

Kin of Astaroth, King of Rot. As a subspecies of the Impure King, her characteristics are similar to his. One of the Impure Clan, she is a pet of the King of Rot.

Evil Ghost

Low to Mid Level

Spirits of wicked intent who harm people, things and environments. Conglomerations of ghosts are especially nasty. Kin of Azazel, King of Spirits.

Shapeshifter

Low to Mid Level

Ghosts that possess semi-solids (water, mud, slime, etc.…in manga, ink) and can take a vague form. Like Evil Ghosts, they are often wicked. Kin of Azazel, King of Spirits.

GALATEA

LOW TO HIGH LEVEL

Demons or Evil Ghosts that take possession of dolls or statues. They are usually low level, but occasionally a high level demon will be one. When that happens, the doll that is the vessel doesn't last long.

FILE 37

YAMANTAKA

HIGH LEVEL

Mysterious Buddhist demons that can appear in Assiah without possessing a material substance in that realm. They are fluids composed of particles known as the Flame of Gehenna and burn the essence of Gehenna itself.

FILE 38

SERAPHIM

MID TO HIGH LEVEL

Kin of Lucifer, King of Light. Souls of light. Only Lucifer can create them. After they appear, they gradually grow hotter until they eventually explode. They convey Lucifer's messages.

BLUE EXORCIST 12

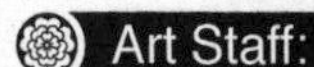

Art Staff:

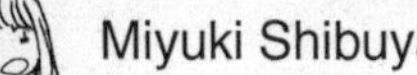

I'M OBSESSED WITH MONHUN!

Miyuki Shibuya

HOW SOOTHING...

Erika Uemura

MITTSU!

Yoshino Kawamura

Art Assistants:

I MOVED.

Hayashi-kun

B'Z!!

Yamanaka-san

FATE/ZERO... LANCER!

Yanagimoto-san

SEMBEI AMBASSADOR.

Yamagishi-san

I'LL GET UP EARLY TOMORROW!

Sakaki-san

Composition Assistant:

I'LL WORK HARD ON YUKIO...

Minoru Sasaki

Kyoto Dialect Advisor

I CAN'T GRASP KONEKOMARU.

Yosuke Takeda

I BROUGHT IN AN ADVISOR FOR THE KYOTO DIALECT IN VOLUME 12!! HE HELPS GIVE EACH OF THE CHARACTERS A DIFFERENT TYPE OF DIALECT!! DIALECTS ARE COMPLICATED!!

Editor

Shihei Rin

Graphic Novel Editor

INCOME COMES AND GOES...

Ryusuke Kuroki

Graphic Novel Design

THEY EVEN DO POSTERS!

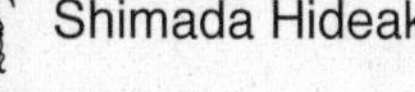

Shimada Hideaki

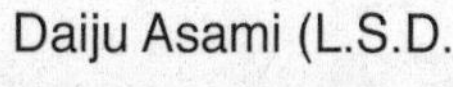

Daiju Asami (L.S.D.)

Manga

Kazue Kato

(in no particular order)
(Note: The caricatures and statements are from memory!)

Because of page limits and schedule issues, there're no question or illustration pages this time! See you in Volume 13!

Yeah, so what!!
You got a problem?!
Izumo, you always look angry. But you're not, right?

※ Izumo Loves Shojo Manga

The new volume of Kimi Monogatari is out!!
GLANCE
GLANCE
No one's at cram school yet, so I'll read it!

!!!
Wait a second...
Huh?!
Ugh...
No way...
Wh... Wh... Whoa...

GYAAAAH
What the?! Unbelievable! Such happiness! Impossible!
Milk

You made my heart skip a beat!
GYAAAAH
YIKES
Milk

Kazue Kato

With volume 12, the story enters a new arc! I planned to draw this story a lot sooner, but it took a long time to get here.

Now dig into volume 12!

BLUE EXORCIST

BLUE EXORCIST VOL. 12
SHONEN JUMP ADVANCED Manga Edition

STORY & ART BY KAZUE KATO

Translation & English Adaptation/John Werry
Touch-up Art & Lettering/John Hunt, Primary Graphix
Cover & Interior Design/Sam Elzway
Editor/Mike Montesa

Printed in the U.S.A.

Published by VIZ Media, LLC
P.O. Box 77010
San Francisco, CA 94107

10 9 8 7 6 5 4 3 2 1
First printing, November 2014

viz
media

www.viz.com

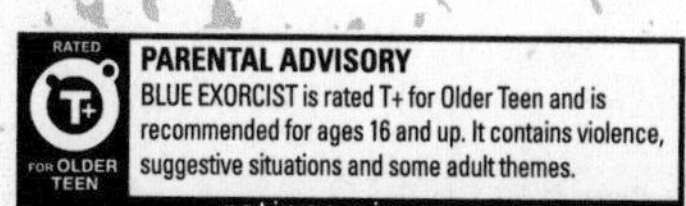
RATED
T+
FOR OLDER TEEN
PARENTAL ADVISORY
BLUE EXORCIST is rated T+ for Older Teen and is recommended for ages 16 and up. It contains violence, suggestive situations and some adult themes.
ratings.viz.com

THE WORLD'S MOST CUTTING-EDGE MANGA
SHONEN JUMP
ADVANCED
www.shonenjump.com

In the next volume...

YOUR MOTHER IS EXPERIMENTAL MATERIAL...
BIBIP
...FOR CREATING AN *ELIXIR* THAT WILL *REVITALIZE* HUMAN CELLS, RESULTING IN *IMMORTALITY.*

The fox god Mike relates the terrible tragedy of Izumo's childhood to the Exwires. The Illuminati's Professor Gedoin, searching for the secret to immortality, subjected Izumo's mother to horrific experiments. When they failed, the Illuminati took Izumo's little sister hostage to force Izumo to do their bidding. Now, Professor Gedoin means to experiment on Izumo herself! Rin and the Exwires aren't about to let that happen and stage a dangerous raid on the massive and mysterious Illuminati fortress, Dream Town Inari! And if they all get out of there alive, will they ever be the same again?

Coming Soon!